For my wife, Rosie,
because nothing would be possible without you

CONTENTS

So, you're going to be a dad...

Whether you've been dreaming of starting a family for years, got lucky on your first try or have been surprised by a happy accident, finding out you're going to be a dad is a huge moment in every man's life and one that should be recognized and celebrated. It really is the most monumental news, so I wanted to kick off this book with heartfelt CONGRATULATIONS from me to you.

Like every new dad who came before you, you're taking a giant leap into the unknown. Your whole life is about to change forever, in countless wonderful and (I won't lie to you) often not-so-wonderful ways. It's a daunting thought. But the fact that you're even reading this, taking the time to inform yourself and prepare for what's to come, is a really positive sign of the kind of dad you want to be. You're already way ahead of the game.

If you're feeling excited, scared, nervous, overwhelmed or a combination of all four, just know that all these feelings are entirely normal, justified and valid.

I always say that fatherhood is a bit like landing the most incredible job of your career. And yet, you're coming into it with no qualifications, no experience and no real clue what the next few months and years have in store. There's so much to get your head around, and you're already on the clock, with less than nine months to get your house in order before the hard work really begins.

It's not going to be easy. Anything worth doing rarely is. The hours are long, the pay is terrible, and you'll be working with someone who doesn't speak your language, needs feeding 8–15 times a day and relies on you to wipe their bum. It's hard work. But, like all jobs, the more you put into it, the more you'll get out of it. And the rewards? Well, they really are huge and will last a lifetime.

As a proud dad of three myself, I can honestly say that fatherhood is one of the best, most rewarding jobs in the world. It's also one of the most important. An opportunity to build a family and shape a whole new life. To pass on your values and everything you've learned to another human being. To change misconceptions and outdated stereotypes. And, ultimately, we all hope, to leave a positive mark on the world.

You'll laugh harder than you ever have before, learn skills you never thought you'd master and fall madly in love with a tiny person you've only just met. Sure, there will be occasions when you find yourself reminiscing about the freedom you had pre-kids. But, in no time at all, you honestly won't be able to imagine your life without them.

I wrote this book as a practical guide for every new dad and carer who wants to play an active role in their child's life. Having written about fatherhood for nearly a decade now, speaking to countless parents and parenting experts along the way, I know first-hand how much conflicting information there is out there for new parents and how difficult it can be to find the advice you need when you need it most. What's more, most of what you'll read about pregnancy and parenthood in other books and online is geared towards mums and their experience, meaning the important role us dads can play is often overlooked.

In these pages, you'll find every single thing I've learned about fatherhood over the years, not just from my own hands-on experience but every great piece of parenting advice, every tip and every trick I've collected from my incredible wife and a whole host of amazing parents around the world who I count as friends, confidantes and co-conspirators.

Whether you read it cover to cover or just dip in and out whenever you need a helping hand, my single biggest hope is that this book will give you a head start on your parenting journey.

My personal promise to you is that I won't sugarcoat things. I'll always be honest with you about how parenting really is (warts and all). And I'm not here to tell you how to be the perfect dad. There really is no such thing, nor is there a magic formula for raising a child. Every baby is unique, and they don't come with an instruction manual (as much as we might wish they did). You'll need to be flexible, try new things and adapt to whatever life throws at you.

You'll make mistakes along the way. We all do. So don't berate yourself too much if you have a bad day or things don't turn out like you planned. Tomorrow is a new day.

All any of us can try to do is figure out how to navigate parenthood in our own way, in the hope we can all give our kids the best start in life. This book will give you the tools to do just that. And if you ever need extra support, have more questions or just want to connect with another dad who's seen it all before, feel free to drop me a message on Instagram @youthedaddy where my DMs are always open, day or night.

Like I said at the start, just by opening this book, you're already way ahead of the game, and I have no doubt that you'll not only be a great dad... you'll absolutely love your new job too. As challenging as it can be, it really is the best one in the world, and your future kid is so lucky to have you.

Foreword by Lindsay Kerrigan,
BSc Midwifery, PgDip Specialist Community Public Health Nursing

Becoming a dad is a life-changing event that will bring so much joy and love. However, it can also be a time that is charged with worry and anxiety.

Having worked in Maternity and Early Years for the past 15 years, I fully understand – and never underestimate – the important role that dads play in this crazy adventure you are about to embark on.

Throughout parenthood, there's always a lot of focus on mother and baby's well-being, and sometimes dads can feel forgotten about and helpless. *You the Daddy* is a brilliant and sometimes laugh-out-loud read that focuses on the impact dads can make while providing reassurance and guidance throughout the early years of your child's life.

Giles Alexander's aim with this book is to give you a leg up in your parenting journey, with his honest words taking you, step by step, through everything he has learned about fatherhood over the years. Each chapter guides you through pregnancy, birth and raising a child, answering all your questions and providing practical tips and advice that will be invaluable for what lies ahead of you.

You the Daddy is definitely the book that all mums-to-be will want their partners to read!

CHAPTER 1

GROWING A BABY

It's funny how the result of a single test can change the course of your life forever. But, from the moment your partner pees on that little stick and it confirms she's pregnant, your life will never be the same again.

The countdown has officially begun. And all being well, in around nine months' time, there will be a brand-new person in the world, relying on you to raise them. There's not a minute to waste – the months will go by in a flash, so it's time to get prepared.

Every new parent starts in the same boat. There's a huge amount to learn, and fast. You'll have to make adjustments to so many aspects of your daily life, from your home and your job to your social life and your priorities. But never forget... as much as you will have to adapt, for the next nine months and beyond, your partner will be the one doing the lion's share.

For all the talk of pregnancy being a magical time, which in many ways it is, more than anything, it's a tough old slog. A marathon of epic proportions. Not only is every mum-to-be physically growing a baby inside her (which is an incredible feat of human biology in itself), her whole life is about to be turned upside down. Anything and everything you can do to make things easier for her during this pregnancy will be your first real test of proving your salt as a father and giving your baby the very best start in life.

In this chapter, we'll cover everything you need to know to survive and thrive during the coming three trimesters of pregnancy. From understanding how your baby is growing and what your partner is going through, to how you can support her, start bonding with your baby and be prepared for every challenge along the way.

This is your time to shine. Your opportunity to step up and be the best pregnancy partner you can possibly be.

A man's guide to baby growth during pregnancy

Once you find out you're going to be a dad, you'll quickly learn that there's a whole new world of pregnancy and parenting knowledge out there that you knew nothing about. Now's the time to inform yourself on what to expect and what your new life will look like.

First things first, download one of the many excellent (and free) pregnancy tracking apps onto your phone. Just plug in the rough date when this baby was "made", and these apps will track your pregnancy in real time, providing useful weekly updates on how your baby is growing and what your partner is going through. Though most of these apps are designed for mums-to-be rather than us dads, you'll still learn a huge amount and reassure your partner by showing how serious you are about supporting her through this pregnancy.

During this early researching phase of fatherhood, some of the very first things you'll come across are baby growth charts, which explain how big your baby is growing week by week by comparing them to different seeds, fruits and vegetables. While these fruity charts start off simply enough, comparing your growing baby to blueberries, strawberries and avocados, before long, they venture into the "exotic aisle" of your local specialist greengrocer. If you struggle to visualize the dimensions of rarely sighted fruit and veg like dragon fruit or acorn squash, these baby growth charts may not be for you.

Instead, let me introduce you to my man's guide to baby growth, which uses universally recognized man-friendly items to help you picture, much more clearly, how big your baby will get over the next 40 weeks. Refer to this over the coming nine months as your partner gets bigger. If nothing else, it will help you truly appreciate what your partner is carrying around with her every day while focusing your mind on the monumental task that awaits her when this baby is ready to be born.

How big is your baby in weeks?

4   5   6   7   8   9   10

11   12   13   14   15   16

17   18   19   20   21   22 to 24

25 to 28   29 to 32   33 to 36   37 to 40

Week 4: full stop (1 mm/0.04 in.)

Week 5: chilli flake (2 mm/0.07 in.)

Week 6: drawing pin (6 mm/0.24 in.)

Week 7: pistachio nut (1.3 cm/0.5 in.)

Week 8: standard washer (1.6 cm/0.6 in.)

Week 9: big toe nail (2.3 cm/0.9 in.)

Week 10: bottle top (3.1 cm/1.2 in.)

Week 11: golf ball (4.1 cm/1.6 in.)

Week 12: your right (bigger) testicle (5.4 cm/2.1 in.)

Week 13: large boiled egg (7.4 cm/2.9 in.)

Week 14: pork pie (8.7 cm/3.4 in.)

Week 15: Scotch egg (10.1 cm/4 in.)

Week 16: light bulb (11.6 cm/4.6 in.)

Week 17: softball (13 cm/5.1 in.)

Week 18: smartphone (14.2 cm/5.6 in.)

Week 19: mini rugby ball (15.3 cm/6 in.)

Week 20: tall pint glass (25.6 cm/10 in.)

Week 21: cordless power drill (26.7 cm/10.5 in.)

Weeks 22–24: bottle of wine (28–30 cm/11–11.8 in.)

Weeks 25–28: UK size 14 man's shoe (34–37 cm/13.4–14.5 in.)

Weeks 29–32: small Halloween pumpkin (38–42 cm/15–16.5 in.)

Weeks 33–36: standard football (43–47 cm/16.9–18.5 in.)

Weeks 37–40: large rugby ball (48–52 cm/18.9–20.5 in.)

Containing your excitement

The early weeks of pregnancy can be a really special time for you and your partner. You're both harbouring a big secret. And, as the only two people in the world to know it, it's entirely up to you when and how you want to share it with the world.

While it might be tempting to shout it from the rooftops and proudly tell everyone your exciting news at the earliest opportunity, many expectant parents choose to hold off sharing it until at least the end of the first trimester, after the 12-week scan.

The principal reason for this is a sad one, but one which all new parents should be aware of. The truth is that miscarriages are more common than most of us think, with around one in four pregnancies not lasting beyond the 12-week stage.

You should know that in the vast majority of cases, miscarriage is unavoidable, the body's way of stopping a pregnancy that has no chance of success. But this doesn't take away from the fact that every experience of baby loss, whenever it occurs, is hugely painful for everyone involved. So, the fewer people you have to inform, should it happen, the fewer times you'll be forced to relive this painful experience.

Positively, the further along your pregnancy is, the lower the risk of miscarriage. After 12 weeks of gestation, the risk of pregnancy loss drops significantly to between 3% and 4%. Once you reach the 20-week mark, the risk is even lower, at around 0.6%. Because of this, most new parents decide to wait until one of these milestones has passed before revealing their big secret to the world.

However, in most cases, this is easier said than done. From around four weeks, your partner may start showing some of the tell-tale signs of pregnancy. Extreme fatigue and morning sickness might make an early appearance, raising eyebrows from anyone who knows you well. Meanwhile, eagle-eyed friends and family may even notice the smallest of changes: your partner's diet, any time she turns down an alcoholic drink or subtly strokes her stomach in a naturally protective, maternal way.

Rationale for telling a few people your news early

The bigger the secret, the harder it is to keep. And, despite my earlier warnings, there are a lot of very good reasons to tell a few discreet people about your pregnancy before your first scan.

If this is your first pregnancy, you and your partner may be feeling anxious about what the coming weeks will bring. Letting a few people in on your secret can provide some much-needed relief. Not just to share in the excitement of what's to come but also to support you, advise you, reassure you and ultimately be there for you should things not work out as planned.

Who to tell

The old friend or sibling who's seen it all before – the more pregnancies they've been through, the better. A great source of advice and wisdom about parenthood and only too happy to share their knowledge with you.

The close work colleague – someone who works with you or your partner, who isn't the office gossip and can be trusted to keep a secret. A valuable support during the working week, covering for your partner if she feels too nauseous to attend a meeting or for you if you need to slip off early for a scan.

The new parents – a reassuring sounding board, they'll have all the best recommendations, most timely tips and (if you're lucky) may even save some of their baby kit and clothes for you to borrow once your little one arrives.

The pregnant friend – ideally a few months further ahead than you, they can pre-warn you of what to expect during every stage of pregnancy while being the emotional support your partner needs when you aren't around.

Understanding what your partner is going through

In the first few weeks of pregnancy, your partner is unlikely to notice any physical symptoms. But, from around four weeks, the pregnancy hormone "human chorionic gonadotropin" will start to kick in, and the early pregnancy symptoms will begin to appear.

They'll usually start small and (on the whole) she'll manage them like a trooper. But as the weeks go by, and the pregnancy symptoms start to pile up, the physical and emotional strain on her will be immense.

The amount of oestrogen and progesterone in her blood will increase by 30–50 times to prepare her body for pregnancy, affecting her mood, causing morning sickness, a constant need to pee and swollen, tender breasts. Her heart will be working 40% harder than yours, contributing again to worsening nausea, painful heartburn and flagging energy levels.

Of course, every pregnancy is different, and every woman's experience is different too. Some will tick off every pregnancy symptom under the sun during the next nine months (see the full checklist on the following pages). Others may only notice a few. And their intensity will be felt differently by different people too.

The only real certainty is that, as the father of this baby, you're the one person in this pregnancy who won't be experiencing any physical changes yourself. She, meanwhile, will go through the wringer and do all the heavy lifting.

DADVICE

As her partner, the better you are at recognizing the different pregnancy symptoms and knowing how to help her manage each of them in turn, the more supported she will feel and the easier this rollercoaster ride will be (head to page 24 for the full lowdown).

Pregnancy symptoms checklist

How mums may feel about pregnancy symptoms	First trimester 1–12 weeks pregnant	Second trimester 13–26 weeks pregnant	Third trimester 27–40 weeks pregnant
Positive	• No period	• No period • Thicker and shinier hair • Morning sickness easing • Feeling baby move for the first time	• No period • Thicker hair • Morning sickness unlikely • Feeling baby's movements
Manageable	• Metallic taste in her mouth • Tiredness • Heightened sense of smell • Craving certain foods	• Weight gain • Nipples may become darker • Fatigue • Appearance of linea nigra (a dark line running from pubic region to her belly button) • Weird cravings	• Weight gain • Low energy levels • Extra smelly farts • Bad breath • Desire to nest • Weird cravings • Extra vaginal discharge
Irritating	• Aversion to certain foods • Needing to pee more often	• Hot flashes • Frequent urination • Constipation • Difficulty sleeping	• Mood swings • Frequent urination (day and night) • Incontinence • Constipation • Difficulty sleeping

How mums may feel about pregnancy symptoms	First trimester 1–12 weeks pregnant	Second trimester 13–26 weeks pregnant	Third trimester 27–40 weeks pregnant
May cause concern	• Light spotting (vaginal bleeding) • Darkened skin or brown patches on her face	• Early appearance of stretch marks • Spider veins on face, arms and legs • Feeling faint/dizzy • Nosebleeds • Anaemia/iron deficiency	• Stretch marks • Anaemia/iron deficiency • Birth anxiety • Shortness of breath • Sore, bleeding gums • Abdominal pains • Braxton Hicks contractions
Unpleasant or painful	• Sore breasts • Nausea • Morning sickness (usually from week six) • Milky white vaginal discharge • Cramping (like period pains) • Bloating	• Sore breasts • More nausea • Morning sickness • Round ligament pain and cramping in groin area • Stiff pelvic joints • Aching around belly • Leg cramps • Back pain • Dry, itchy skin • Haemorrhoids • Heartburn • Palpitations	• Aching breasts • Varicose veins • Swollen feet and ankles • Swollen vagina • Leg cramps • Back pain • Rib pain • Hormonal imbalance • Dry, itchy skin • Haemorrhoids • Heartburn • Palpitations

When to seek professional help

If this is your first baby, every new pregnancy symptom and every new ache and pain can make you want to sound the alarm bells. While there is usually nothing to worry about, don't put off asking for help if something doesn't feel right. Trust your partner's instincts and trust your own too.

While friends and family can be great sources of reassurance during pregnancy, they (usually) aren't medical professionals, so be careful whose advice you take. The same applies to looking up scary symptoms on the internet – you'll often find conflicting advice or horror stories that send you down the wrong path.

Contact your doctor or midwife if:

- A pain or symptom is especially intense or doesn't go away.

- Your partner has a burning sensation when she pees or notices blood in her urine – she may have a urinary tract infection (UTI).

- She experiences vaginal bleeding at any stage during the pregnancy.

- Your baby is usually active, but your partner hasn't felt them move for a day or so (try waking up the baby first, though – getting your partner to walk around, have a relaxing bath, drink ice cold water or crunch on some ice cubes usually does the trick).

- Your partner experiences a sudden swelling in the face, feet or hands – all symptoms of pre-eclampsia (a rare but potentially dangerous blood pressure condition that shouldn't be ignored).

- She suddenly has problems with her vision or starts vomiting during the third trimester.

Nine times out of ten, it will be a false alarm, but it's better to know for certain than to risk your baby's or your partner's health.

Emotional pressures on mums-to-be

Though your partner may not experience any physical pregnancy symptoms right away, the emotional pressures of pregnancy will begin weighing on her mind the moment she finds out she's expecting.

These pressures won't ease as she moves through this pregnancy. Her worry list will keep stacking up all the way until the birth, after which a whole new set of emotional stresses will take over. You'll no doubt be feeling many of these too, but never underestimate just how much pressure your partner will personally be feeling right now.

Keep this in mind at all times over the coming months and years, and make it your mission to share the load however you can (while trying your best not to add to her worry list).

- Discuss both of your career ambitions and personal goals and figure out a way forward together.
- Listen when she shares her worries and act on them.
- Try not to say you'll do something then let it slip your mind.
- Don't leave all the baby admin until the last minute, assuming she'll handle it.

You made this baby together and it is only fair that the responsibilities of parenthood should be a partnership too.

A snapshot of her worry list

Will I be a good mother?

How can I keep this baby alive?

What if something goes wrong?

Are these pregnancy symptoms normal?

Why can't I feel the baby moving?

Is the baby moving around too much?

What if I can't breastfeed?

Will people judge me if we formula feed?

When is my next scan?

What if the scan shows something wrong with our baby?

What supplements should I be taking?

Have I taken my supplements?

Am I doing too much/too little exercise?

Why are maternity clothes so expensive?

What pre-natal classes do I need to book?

Should I do hypnobirthing?

What if the baby is born prematurely?

Am I strong enough to cope with the labour?

What do I need to pack in my hospital bag?

Should I have an epidural?

Will I poo during the birth?

What if something goes wrong and we can't follow our birth plan?

What if I tear during the birth?

Could the birth make me incontinent?

What if I don't immediately bond with this baby?

What if I need a caesarean?

What baby kit do we need to buy?

What pram do we need?

Should we use reusable or disposable nappies?

How are we going to decorate the nursery?

How will we afford it all?

How will we cope when the baby arrives?

What if I get postnatal depression?

How will this baby affect our relationship?

Will sex be the same afterwards?

Will my partner still find me attractive?

Will I ruin my vagina giving birth?

Why can't I control my emotions?

How will this baby affect my friendships?

Will my body ever be the same again?

Will anyone want to hang out with me after I've had the baby?

How can we afford to live when I'm on maternity leave?

Will I still have a job when it's time to go back to work?

Will people judge me if I go back to work?

How will motherhood affect my career?

Who will look after the baby when I go back to work?

DADVICE

Many of the answers to these questions will become clearer as your pregnancy develops or when your baby is born. Some you can influence, while others will come down to fate. Just remember that so much of parenthood is unpredictable. We're all just learning as we go, so try not to worry about things that are outside your control. What will be, will be.

Supporting your partner during pregnancy

With so many pregnancy symptoms to manage, it can be hard to know where your support can make the biggest difference. The most useful thing you can do is learn what symptoms to look out for and how to (at least partially) ease them. Though your actions won't prevent each symptom from occurring, they will at least show your partner that you understand what she's going through and that you're in this together. Let's take each one in turn...

Morning sickness

- Don't be fooled by the name. Morning sickness can strike at any time, day or night, most commonly when your partner's stomach is either empty or too full.

- When cooking or ordering in, avoid rich foods and large portion sizes.

- Remind your partner to stay well hydrated and ensure you have a good supply of plain snacks in the cupboard – simple biscuits and crackers are a winner – leaving some on her bedside table or packing them in her bag before she goes to work, as a pick-me-up during the day.

- If things get really rough and she's vomiting daily, this can be a real downer for her, so try to be around and available when her nausea is worst, both for emotional support and to take on more while she's suffering.

DID YOU KNOW?

Around 3% of pregnant women suffer from an intense form of morning sickness called hyperemesis gravidarum, which causes severe vomiting that can lead to rapid weight loss, extreme dehydration and, if untreated, depression and tears to the oesophagus. Speak to your doctor if you are worried about this. While there are drugs she can take to relieve the symptoms (which usually ease off by week 20), around one in five expectant mums with severe hyperemesis will have these debilitating symptoms throughout their whole pregnancy.

Aversion to certain foods

- Keep a running log of foods that she enjoys and can hold down versus those that make her nauseous. It's likely that this list will evolve week by week, so you both need to keep on top of it.

- Some pregnant women can develop an aversion to protein-rich foods like meat, poultry and fish. This can be an issue as protein is critical for your baby's growth, with expecting mums needing more of it in their diet (around 60–100 grams daily). If this happens, experiment with plant-based protein alternatives or try serving up the food she's avoiding in a different texture, temperature or consistency.

- Avoid cooking anything with a strong smell at home as the scent can linger in the air or on your clothes and soft furnishings, triggering her nausea long after you've eaten.

Low energy

- Growing a baby is a huge physical undertaking that will zap her energy levels and make everyday tasks feel like a huge effort. So give her a chance to put her feet up during the evenings and weekends.

- Limit late-night social plans and make it a priority for you both to go to bed early (by 10 p.m. latest) to give you both some much-needed downtime and optimize your sleep cycles before the baby arrives.

- Expectant mums need to drink a lot during pregnancy, so help her stay well hydrated. Avoid too many fizzy drinks or traditional teas/ coffees as they contain caffeine, which can be harmful to the baby if she has too much of it. Herbal teas, water and squash are generally your best bet.

- If she's feeling particularly drained, chances are she's low in iron. Buy natural iron supplements for her to take and cook more iron-rich foods at home, like red meat, kale and spinach. It's worth being aware that taking iron supplements can cause constipation.

Constipation

- Laxatives aren't recommended during pregnancy, so she'll need to stick with natural remedies to help her feel more comfortable.

- Help her stay well hydrated, increase the amount of high-fibre foods (like kidney beans, lentils, oats, chia seeds, fruit and vegetables) in her diet and take regular exercise together to help get things moving again. Prunes and prune juice are both highly effective too.

Difficulty sleeping

- Expectant mums are advised to sleep on their side, as lying on their back or front can be harmful to the baby. If this isn't your partner's usual sleeping position, chances are she won't sleep as well as usual.

- Buy a pregnancy pillow. These are specially designed to perfectly mould to the shape of a woman's body during pregnancy, whatever position she's lying in, providing the ultimate support for her bump, legs and back. They are also useful for long drives in the car, getting comfortable on the sofa and as a breastfeeding pillow.

- If you are a snorer, invest in some snoring strips, switch up your own sleeping position to limit your snoring and don't be offended if she asks you to sleep on the sofa every once in a while.

Aches and pains

- Ibuprofen is not advised during pregnancy, so stick with paracetamol for pain relief.

- Embrace the magic of massage. Buy some pregnancy-safe massage oil and offer her a massage whenever she complains of soreness. Since pregnant women shouldn't lie on their stomach or flat on their back from 20 weeks of gestation, back massages are best done with her lying on her side or sitting front to back on a chair.

- During the colder months, provide a constant supply of hot water bottles to keep her and the baby warm while soothing her aching muscles.

- Some expectant mums also experience leg cramps, which usually strike at night, so be responsible for massaging the affected area whenever cramp strikes. Regular light exercise and stretching before bed can help reduce the regularity of these.

Swollen feet and ankles

- Encourage her to put her feet up as often as she can, even if this means you need to take on more of the hard graft at home.

- Avoid long walks or social plans that don't involve lots of opportunities to sit down and rest.

- Get into the habit of offering your partner regular foot rubs at the end of each day. For best results, don't always wait to be asked.

Itchy skin and stretch marks

- Buy some special mum-to-be moisturizing lotion or oil early in pregnancy to rub on her tummy and legs, as they can reduce itchiness and the severity of stretch marks.

- Reassure her that stretch marks tend to fade slowly after your baby is born, but even if they don't, they are positive marks of motherhood and in no way make you see her any differently.

Low mood

- Remind her to take her pregnancy supplements every day. Deficiencies in minerals such as iron and zinc have both been linked to depression, so it's best to make sure she's topped up.

- Mood swings are common in pregnancy, but even if you're expecting them, they still can be difficult to take on the chin. Just remember this is the woman you love and the future mother of your child, so bite your tongue and try to absorb any seemingly unfair outbursts over the coming months.

- Exercise is great at lifting the mood (it's advised that pregnant women should get at least 150 minutes of moderate aerobic activity every week), though she may not always have the energy. Encourage her to sign up for low-impact workouts like Pilates, swimming or pregnancy yoga and offer to go for walks together.

Abdominal pains

- Since your baby is growing at a phenomenal rate, your partner may feel pains in her abdomen, which can be extremely worrying for both of you. These are usually entirely normal, most commonly "round ligament pain" caused by the stretching of the ligaments that hold her uterus in place.

- To help minimize these pains, run her a hot bath, bring her hot water bottles to hold on her tummy or buy her a pregnancy belt (a specialist piece of kit which can provide extra support for her bump).

- While this symptom is common, do encourage her to talk it through with her doctor, midwife or a maternity physiotherapist if she's worried. It's always better to be safe than sorry.

Hot flashes

- An increase in blood supply to the skin and hormonal changes during pregnancy can cause your partner to feel uncomfortably hot and sweaty during certain parts of her pregnancy.

- Turn the thermostat down and invest in a fan or air-conditioning unit for your bedroom.

- Provide her with a steady supply of cool drinks and keep your ice trays constantly topped up in the freezer.

- On warm nights, delivering a cold flannel or ice pack to her bedside will always go down a treat.

Haemorrhoids

- Very common during pregnancy, especially if your partner is suffering from regular constipation, haemorrhoids (also known as piles) are enlarged blood vessels inside the rectum or around the anus, which can be extremely uncomfortable and painful.

- While they should get better on their own in a few days, treating them at the first sign of discomfort can help keep them under control.

- Save her embarrassment at the pharmacy by going to buy haemorrhoid cream for her.

- Encourage her to sit down more, as standing for long periods of time is one of the causes. Warm baths are effective at relieving some of the pain too.

Braxton Hicks contractions

- These "false" or "practice" contractions are entirely normal, usually occurring throughout the third trimester to help prepare new mums' muscles for labour. As common as they are, they can be very worrying for first-time mums, so learn how to recognize the difference between Braxton Hicks contractions and true labour contractions.

- As a general rule, Braxton Hicks contractions arrive at irregular intervals and often go away when your partner moves or changes positions. By contrast, real labour contractions arrive at regular intervals and get closer together and stronger over time.

- When any contraction starts – whether real or false – track their timings to measure how long they last and how regular they are. You'll quickly notice a pattern if there is one.

Feeling overwhelmed

- With so much to organize before the baby arrives, don't leave all the baby admin to your partner. Do your own research so you know what to buy and when (jump to pages 41–46 for more advice on this), step up and do the DIY you've been putting off and research classes you both should take to prepare you for the birth and parenthood.

- Forgetfulness (sometimes referred to as "baby brain") is common during pregnancy and early motherhood. Create a shared calendar on both of your phones and put another on your wall at home, to ensure neither of you forgets your upcoming midwife appointments, scans, classes and other commitments.

- Limit financial worries by starting to save now while planning ahead for how you'll both manage your finances during parental leave (and further ahead if one of you plans to stay at home to look after the baby).

- Look into what paternity benefits you have at work and consider how you might change your job or the hours you work once the baby is born so that you can be more available at home.

Take some of the stress out of her daily routine by making your partner a pregnancy survival kit to take to work. Include her pregnancy supplements (so she never forgets to take them), a bottle of water (to stay hydrated), healthy snacks (to keep her blood sugar level up), gel in-soles, plasters and flip-flops (for when her shoes get too uncomfortable), paracetamol (for unexpected pregnancy pains) and emergency loo roll (for urgent, unplanned visits to the nearest bathroom).

Restricted movement

- As she gets bigger, she may depend on you more than ever to help with certain tasks, so always be on call and willing to help.

- Hold doors open for her, carry her bag and (most useful of all) help put her shoes on in the morning (a very difficult task for her to do alone with a huge baby bump in the way).

Feeling insecure

- With her body changing and hormones raging, she may well not be feeling her normal, confident self, which might make her question how much support she's getting from you or the strength of your relationship.

- Help ease any worries by reminding her daily how beautiful she is, what incredible strength she's showing during this pregnancy and how much you love her.

- As her pregnancy progresses and she feels increasingly bloated, gassy and sleep deprived, with a growing bump, sore breasts and even a swollen vagina, sex may well be the last thing on her mind. Be sensitive to this and don't put pressure on her. Remember, there are lots of other ways to show intimacy – taking her out for dinner, a hug, a kiss or being the big spoon for the night will go a long way.

Pregnancy scans – what to expect

You'll be offered various ultrasound scans or sonograms at key stages of your pregnancy to check your baby is developing as they should. These are most commonly offered between weeks 10 and 14 of pregnancy (known as the dating scan) and again at around weeks 18 to 21 (known as the anomaly scan, when you can usually find out the sex, too, if you'd like). However, if you want to see more of your baby on screen or have any worries, you can pay for additional scans yourself at any stage.

If your partner has experienced miscarriages or baby loss previously, is over 35 (sometimes referred to by doctors as a "geriatric mother") or has any medical conditions that could pose risks to her or the baby, your doctor may suggest an earlier scan at around 6–8 weeks, and more regular scans throughout the pregnancy to make sure everything is on track.

Whatever your situation, each scan brings with it a huge mix of emotions: from excitement and anticipation at finally getting the chance to see your baby, hear the heartbeat and get confirmation that all is well to fear, worry and anxiety at what the scan might reveal.

It's important, as the father of this baby, that you make it a priority to attend every check-up and scan with your partner, to be by her side and provide the support she needs in this moment. They're also a great opportunity to build a connection with your baby and ask the professionals in the room any questions you might have.

Every scan involves a lot of petroleum jelly and prodding of your partner's belly, which can be uncomfortable for her. They usually last around an hour, though you should allow extra time. Sometimes your baby is in the wrong position or moving around too much, which can delay things. And don't be concerned if the sonographer is a bit quiet during the scan itself. They will be busy locating and measuring all your baby's vital organs, bones and joints to make sure each one is present and the right size.

Dating scan (10–14 weeks)

- Your partner will need a full bladder for best results.

- The ultrasound technician is looking for a strong heartbeat, correct blood flow, and some movement, with early indications of their developing organs, spine and brain.

- If your baby is in the wrong position, your partner might be asked to stand up and jiggle around so they can try and get a better angle.

Mid-pregnancy scan (18–21 weeks)

- Also known as the anomaly or viability scan. While the chances of miscarriage after this stage of pregnancy are much smaller, this scan provides your midwife with a fuller picture of your baby's health and development, checking everything from bone and organ development to blood flow within your baby's heart.

- The scan will also check for various rare conditions, such as spina bifida (a defect in the baby's spine and spinal cord) and cleft lip.

- While you can usually find out the sex of your baby during this scan (if you'd like to know in advance), don't go into the appointment expecting to find out for certain, as sometimes it can't be confirmed at this stage (depending on if the baby is in the right position or not). If you really don't want to find out the sex, remind the ultrasound technician to ask you to look away at the pivotal moment to avoid any unplanned flashes of the genitals on screen.

Late pregnancy check-ups (third trimester)

- As you approach your due date, ultrasound scans are less common, unless your doctor or midwife has any concerns.

- In most cases, late pregnancy appointments will involve simpler checks of the baby's heart rate and your partner's general health (taking her blood pressure and getting urine samples).

Connecting with your baby (from the outside)

While most new mothers feel a deep physical connection with the little person growing inside them, the same can't always be said for new dads. We're on the outside. Our bodies aren't changing to accommodate a new life. We can't feel them moving around in our bellies. And we aren't the ones who are physically going to give birth when the time comes.

Because of this, lots of dads can feel somewhat disconnected during pregnancy. While you might assume that every new parent feels an instant connection with their baby, this isn't always the case. Connections take time to develop, especially when you've never actually met the person you're building a relationship with. But you don't have to wait until your baby is born to start bonding with them...

First kick

From around the halfway point of pregnancy, your partner should start to feel the baby moving around. Initially, only she will feel these flutters. But, before long, these movements will become bigger kicks that you can feel from the outside too. Take every opportunity to put your hand or cheek on your partner's bump when she tells you the baby's kicking. I guarantee you'll never have wanted to be kicked in the face more.

Seeing is believing

Try to attend every ultrasound appointment to see your baby on screen. Each one is special, an opportunity to see how your baby is growing and morphing from an unidentifiable object into a real little person. Keep the scan photos in your wallet and proudly show them off to anyone willing to look. You'll feel like a proper dad before you know it.

Baby talk

Towards the end of the second trimester, your baby should be able to hear sounds from the outside world, including your voice. It might feel silly, but try talking or singing to your partner's bump whenever you get the chance, as it can help build an early connection. Studies have also shown this can help your baby recognize your voice sooner after they're born.

CHAPTER 2

PREPARING FOR YOUR NEW ARRIVAL

Once you've reached the halfway point of pregnancy, it's time to start thinking about your birth plan and what you'll need to buy for when your baby arrives. It can be tempting to start this process as soon as you find out you're pregnant, but I'd strongly recommend holding off at least until you've had your 20-week scan when you'll have a bit more certainty that everything is progressing as it should.

Again, there are so many things to consider and still more to learn. While you may have already mastered being a supportive pregnancy partner to your growing other half, it's now time to get up to speed on the birth and your first few months of parenthood.

From the third trimester, new opportunities will open up for you to join parenting groups, meet your doctors or midwives and attend breastfeeding clinics. As you near your due date, I urge you to attend as many of these as you can with your partner (yes, even the breastfeeding clinics), as the better informed you are, the more helpful you can be down the line.

My best advice, though, is to try and be fully ready, with everything in place for your new arrival, at least a month before your due date.

You'll hear from various well-intentioned people throughout your pregnancy that it's very common for firstborn babies to arrive late, but that really is just an old wives' tale. Our first gave us the surprise of our lives when he arrived a month early, and we were nowhere near as prepared as we wanted to be. Try not to make the same mistake we did; it piled on a load of extra stress and worry at the start of our parenting life, which every knackered new parent can do without.

You're nearly there now. So, keep up the great work, stay positive and keep your eyes on the prize. Just one final push and you'll soon have a beautiful new baby in your arms that you can call your own.

Making a birth plan

After you've had your mid-pregnancy scan, sit down with your partner to discuss her birth plan. A birth plan is a set of preferences for how she'd like the birth of your baby to go, from the location and environment she wants to create during labour to how much intervention she's willing to accept from the doctors and nurses. Keep in mind that these should be preferences, not certainties... birth is unpredictable and rarely goes exactly according to plan, so you'll need to bake in some flexibility and be open to compromise when the time comes (see page 79 for more details).

Things to decide in advance

Where – Hospital or home birth?

Who – Who does she want in the room during the birth? You/another birth partner/a doula (specialist birthing companion)?

Environment – Music or quiet space? Dimly lit? Diffuser with essential oils?

Type of birth – Vaginal or planned caesarean (usually only advised for specific medical reasons)? Water birth/on bed/off bed? Hypnobirthing?

Intervention – Is she willing for the doctor or midwife to use medical instruments like forceps or a ventouse/suction cup to deliver the baby? Or do an episiotomy (an incision made to the perineum during childbirth) if they need to get the baby out quickly? Whatever you decide, keep in mind that, in certain circumstances, interventions like these may be needed to save both mum and baby's life, so should never be ruled out entirely.

Pain relief – Nothing/paracetamol/TENS machine/gas and air/ diamorphine/epidural?

Guided pushing – Does she want the midwife to guide her through the final stages of labour and/or support the baby's head through the crowning stage (which can reduce the risk of vaginal tearing)?

Delayed cord clamping – Known as "wait for white", some parents choose after the birth to delay clamping and cutting the umbilical cord until it stops pulsating and turns white. This usually takes just a few minutes and means your baby gets all the blood it needs from the placenta. Be aware, in an emergency, this won't always be possible.

Gender reveal – Do you want the midwife to reveal the baby's sex when they're born, or would you rather discover it for yourselves in your own time?

Vitamin K injection – After the birth, you will be offered an injection of vitamin K for your baby, as this helps prevent a rare bleeding disorder called hemorrhagic disease of the newborn. While this injection is highly recommended, some parents decline it as they don't like the thought of injecting their baby so soon after birth.

Delivering the placenta – After your baby is born, your partner will still need to deliver the placenta, which has been keeping your baby alive for the past nine months. To do this, your partner can choose from the following options:

- Active management – where she receives an injection of oxytocin into her thigh after the birth to make her womb contract and deliver the placenta faster. It lowers the risk of postpartum haemorrhage (heavy bleeding after birth) but can cause additional nausea and make your partner's afterpains (contraction-like pains after birth) worse.

- Physiological management – where she has no intervention and lets everything happen naturally (which can take up to an hour but often a lot less).

DID YOU KNOW?

Many mums today are choosing to eat their placenta after birth, either by turning it into smoothies (blending small chunks with fruit and juice) or through placenta encapsulation (where the placenta is dried, powdered and turned into pills to swallow). Though the benefits aren't scientifically proven, fans of this believe consuming the placenta can help increase milk supply, balance hormones and lower the chances of postnatal depression. If your partner wants to try this, look into getting the placenta professionally prepped and make sure your midwife knows your plan so that they store the placenta correctly after birth.

Once you've written everything down, save your birth plan on your phone or print out a copy to put in your hospital bag.

Introduction to hypnobirthing

If your partner is feeling anxious about giving birth, unsure how she will get through it or deal with the pain of labour, hypnobirthing could be the answer.

First things first, hypnobirthing has nothing to do with being "hypnotized". It is a long-established antenatal programme designed to release fear, build confidence during labour and provide you and your partner with the knowledge and techniques you need for a more comfortable, calm and positive birth experience.

If this sounds too good to be true, you aren't the first to think that. Most new dads start off as sceptics when hypnobirthing is first brought up. But if you look into it properly, you'll quickly appreciate just how much about hypnobirthing makes sense.

Addressing the culture of fear surrounding birth

Hypnobirthing is about training the mind to think about birth and "pain" differently. There is so much fear that surrounds giving birth, made worse by exaggerated depictions of childbirth on TV and horror stories passed down through the generations. Even the language around childbirth – like "going into labour" and "contractions" – conjures up images of pain and suffering. It's no wonder that most new mums' minds are loaded with fear and negative preconceptions as they approach their due date.

When it comes to childbirth, fear is a mother's worst enemy as it makes her body release adrenaline, which slows and can ultimately halt the progress of birth. But when fear is removed, her body produces endorphins – the feel-good hormones – which prevent the production of adrenaline and other stress hormones and should help a mother have a shorter and more comfortable birth experience.

Part of the hypnobirthing training involves changing the narrative around childbirth and using different language – for example, talking about "powerful surges" rather than "painful contractions". Another key element is removing fear from the process by surrounding yourselves with positive birth stories and avoiding reading, watching or listening to negative ones.

Affirmations and the important role dads can play

Positive birth affirmations play a big role in hypnobirthing and can be incredibly powerful for boosting your partner's birthing confidence. These affirmations – usually provided as scripts for you to read to your partner – help her visualize the different stages of birth and what her body is experiencing while giving you a clear role in helping her have the positive birth she wants.

By learning about hypnobirthing together, you will play an integral part in preparing your partner to give birth, practising the techniques and working on the affirmation scripts together. You will get to know her birth plan and preferences intimately, learning exactly what to say to reassure her and help her stay calm, relaxed and focused when the time comes.

Being prepared for anything

One of the key benefits of hypnobirthing is that it can be used in any birthing scenario, keeping you and your partner focused and relaxed even if your birth plan changes unexpectedly. No two births are the same, and sometimes, you might need to change your plan for the safety of your partner or your baby. Hypnobirthing gives you the techniques to stay calm and avoid fear in any situation.

DADVICE

It's never too late to learn hypnobirthing, but it's recommended that you start around the halfway point of pregnancy (the longer you have to practise the techniques, the better). To get started, order *The Hypnobirthing Book* by Katharine Graves, which will teach you everything you need to know. You can also take online or in-person hypnobirthing classes if you're short on time or if your budget allows.

Antenatal classes and new parent groups

There are countless tutorials, classes and groups available for expectant parents who want some help preparing for birth and early parenthood. These can be broad in subject matter, covering everything from how to have a healthy pregnancy through to the birth and looking after a newborn. Others can be more targeted, focused on specific skills like pregnancy exercises, pregnancy massage, relaxation methods, birthing techniques and breastfeeding.

If you live in a city or highly populated area and want to benefit from the social aspect of classes and groups, it's likely you'll have lots of options on your doorstep. If you live somewhere more rural, it can be trickier, so be prepared that you might have to travel to take part in a class or pick one that allows virtual participation. Generally, these classes come at a cost, but speak to your local hospital to find out if there are any free classes in your local area.

Most antenatal classes and new parent groups start around 8–10 weeks before your baby is due, which means everyone you meet will be expecting around the same time as you. If you're expecting twins, it's recommended that you start these classes a little earlier – usually around 24 weeks pregnant – as twins are more likely to be born early.

Tips for getting the most out of these classes

- Make every effort to attend – while some classes will appear to be targeted at mums, you will still get a huge amount out of them.

- Take copious notes and re-read them afterwards.

- Do your own research before each class and come armed with a list of questions you want to ask during each session.

- Don't be afraid to ask silly questions. If you're embarrassed to ask in front of everyone, hang back at the end and ask the teacher.

- Try to make friends with the other couples in the group. They know exactly what you're going through and can form part of your support network after your babies are born.

What to buy in advance of baby's arrival

If you search online, you will be confronted by countless lists of essential baby items that you simply "have to buy" before your little one's arrival. But be wary of what you read online – many of these lists are written by companies who have a vested interest in encouraging you to buy what they're selling.

Instead, stick to the following lists, which have been designed to accommodate a range of budgets and lifestyles. While you'll probably want to buy most things new if this is your first baby, don't be afraid of going second-hand (for literally anything apart from car seats and cot mattresses, which should always be bought new). With a bit of effort, you can often find pre-loved bargains that are as good as new.

Pregnancy, birth and postpartum essentials

- Pregnancy pillow – to support your partner's bump during the final stages of pregnancy
- Maternity clothes – to ensure she feels as comfortable as possible
- Incontinence bed pads – to lie on during late pregnancy and after your baby is born
- Ibuprofen and paracetamol – to help with pain relief during her recovery period
- Maternity pants and extra absorbent pads – to cope with the extra blood loss she'll experience in the weeks after the birth
- Specialist moisturizer or skin oil – to reduce scarring from stretch marks, tears or C-section incisions
- Reusable breast pads, compresses and nipple cream – essential if she plans on breastfeeding
- Nursing bras and tops – for easy access (and comfort) when breastfeeding and pumping

Newborn kit list

	Essentials (quantities are the minimum you'll need)	Nice to have (if you have the budget and space at home)
Clothing	• 6 x cotton short-sleeved bodysuits/vests (buy sizes newborn and 0–3 months in case you have a bigger baby) • 6 x cotton babygrows/sleepsuits with enclosed feet and poppers or zips • 2 x cotton hats to keep their head warm • 3 x cardigans (knitted cotton or wool, ideally) • 6 x cotton bibs	• Extra outfits (depending on your personal style) • 2 x wool hats • 2 x pairs of knitted booties • 2 x scratch mittens (if your babygrows don't have enclosed hands)
Changing	• Lots of nappies (newborn and next size up) – if using disposable, have at least 30; if going reusable, have at least 15 to start with (see page 106) • Cotton wool (for cleaning their bum and umbilical cord stump) • Nappy rash cream • Changing mat • Nappy bags (only if using disposable nappies)	• Changing table (comfortable height to save your back) • Towels or cover for changing mat

Feeding	• 6 x muslins/burping cloths • Comfortable chair for feeding • Nursing pillow If planning to bottle feed (buy later if unsure): • 6 x bottles (glass or plastic) with newborn teats • Sterilizer (a microwaveable one is best if you're short on space) • Baby bottle brush	• Breast pump
Sleeping	• 4 x swaddles/large muslins • 2 x cellular blankets • Moses basket (with new mattress) • 3 x fitted cotton sheets • Room thermometer	• Baby monitor (audio or video, depending on budget) • White noise machine
Other kit	• Baby changing bag (any good-sized bag will do) • Pram (with bassinet or lie flat option) • Newborn car seat (avoid second-hand) • Bath seat • Baby sponge/flannel • 2 x baby towels • Saline drops (for clearing blocked noses)	• Baby bouncer • Baby bath • Bath thermometer • Digital ear thermometer • Baby carrier or sling

Things you won't need right away

- Teddies – save these for later, as newborns shouldn't sleep with any unnecessary items in their bed.

- Comforters – used as sleeping aids for your baby once they're a little older, often becoming their go-to toy or comfort blanket for years to come. Once they've chosen a clear favourite, buy a spare in case you lose one or need to put one in the wash.

- Toys and rattles – not needed until they're a bit more interactive.

- Baby mobile – to hang above their changing mat or above their cot once they move into their own room.

- Playmat/baby gym – useful as a safe place to put your baby down and encourage independent play, but not until they're a bit bigger.

- Travel cot – essential if you're planning on going away for the night or on holiday, but best to use your Moses basket for the first two months as a safer option.

DADVICE

Aim to be ready for your new arrival at least a month before your due date. While you and your partner will be focused on the specific date you've been given, remember this is just a statistical best guess. In reality, the normal range for a baby to be born is anywhere between 37 to 42 weeks of gestation; however, it's not uncommon for babies to be born prematurely (between 24 to 37 weeks of gestation).

Choosing the perfect pram

Buying your baby's first pram is a big deal. This essential piece of kit will become part of the furniture at home, being used by you and your partner almost every day and literally coming everywhere with you for the next couple of years. It's also a big investment, so you'll want to make sure it fits with your lifestyle and budget, and that it lasts (especially if you plan on having more than one baby).

There are hundreds of different makes and models you can choose, so don't rush into a purchase that you might regret later. Do your research. Consider how the pram will fit into your home, your car and your daily life. Ask friends with babies what pram they chose and how much they like it. And give your favourite options a test run in the shop to make sure they live up to your expectations (even if you end up buying online). Here's what you need to consider:

How versatile is it?

Newborns should never lie down on an incline or sit up in a pram or buggy, so whichever one you choose needs to have a "lie-flat" option. Ideally, buy a pram that is versatile and can be adjusted for the age of your baby, with a bassinet attachment or lie-flat option for when they are little and a separate tilting seat attachment or functionality for when they get bigger. It's nice to have the option to attach your car seat to the pram frame, but it's only really useful if your baby will sleep in its car seat (which isn't recommended for more than two hours, in any case). Plus, if you're planning on having more than one baby in the next couple of years, you might want to consider a pram with a double (toddler and baby) seat option.

How big is it?

Prams come in all shapes and sizes, so be meticulous in knowing the measurements of your favourite options, both when in use and folded away. It needs to be able to fit through your front door and corridors and be easy to store at home or in your car without getting in the way. If you're tall, make sure the height of the handlebars is adjustable and comfortable for you to avoid back-ache.

How heavy is it?

Chances are, you will need to carry this pram up and down stairs and in and out of the house and car/public transport a lot over the coming years, so its weight is an important factor to consider. While lightweight is good for your back, you do want some substance to your pram to ensure it doesn't tip over easily (especially when you attach a heavy changing bag or your shopping to the handlebars).

How does it look?

Light colours may appeal, but they age quickly and get dirty easily, so darker colours are often a safer option. If your pram doesn't come with a waterproof canopy attachment, invest in one, as this will be essential to avoid your baby getting soaked through if you're ever caught out in the rain.

How much storage does it have?

Any time you leave the house with your baby, you'll need to bring a lot of kit with you (from nappies, wipes and changes of clothes to bottles, toys and bibs). Generally, the more storage your pram provides, the better, so check out the capacity of the basket underneath the seat to ensure it is suitably generous.

How does it fit with your lifestyle?

Where and how you live, day to day, will determine what kind of pram you should get. If you live in the countryside or are very active and outdoorsy, consider a three-wheeler pram with large, pumpable tyres that can handle any terrain. If you live in the city, you might prefer a smaller, nimbler model that can navigate tight corners, busy pavements and public transport.

Nesting and setting up your nursery

Nesting isn't something most men are wired to do, so it may seem like an odd concept – but it's entirely natural for expectant mothers to suddenly get the urge to clean, organize and create a comfortable "nest" at home as they near their due date. So, if you find your partner making lists, painting a wall, clearing out cupboards or asking you to put up shelves in the middle of the night, don't be concerned – this is just their natural nesting instinct kicking in.

A good way to channel this energy is to focus on setting up your baby's nursery. While it's not recommended that your newborn actually sleeps in this room during the night until they are at least six months old, the nursery can still be a functional and calming space at home to feed, change and play with your baby during their early months. So, it's good to have this all set up before your baby arrives while you still have the time and energy to decorate it.

Things to consider

- Deep clean the room first – hoover well and wipe down all the surfaces with an antibacterial spray.

- If painting, make sure you do this well in advance of your baby's arrival, as the fumes from the paint aren't good for their little lungs.

- You'll be spending a lot of time in this room over the coming years, so prioritize comfort over style. If you have the space, include a comfortable chair for night feeds and a small table next to it, so you have somewhere to put a drink, snack or your phone while feeding your baby.

- Think about the lighting – you'll want soft lighting options (like a night light) for when you're changing a nappy or feeding during the small hours of the night.

- Make sure it's a functional space, with lots of storage for your baby's clothes and kit, all within reaching distance of your changing station (see page 103) that's fully stocked with all the nappies, wipes, creams and cotton wool you'll possibly need.

- Temperature control is so important in the nursery as a baby's room should be kept between 16 and 20°C (60 and 68°F), so invest in a fan or heater to help with that.

- Don't stress if you don't have a cot when your baby arrives. For the first six months or so, your baby will sleep in a Moses basket or bassinet in your room, not the nursery, so this big purchase can wait.

- If you want to put up a cot and baby mobile now, put an extra hook in the ceiling above your changing table and hang the mobile there for the time being. It will be a great distraction to keep your baby entertained while you're changing their nappy.

- Organize your new baby clothes into age groups (newborn sizes together and 0–3 month sizes in a different pile) and have an empty storage box or basket to put clothes in that they've grown out of. They go through sizes very quickly in their first year, and it's hard to keep track.

- Finally, don't put off DIY jobs until the last minute – once your baby arrives, you likely won't have the time or the energy to complete them, so best get these out of the way early.

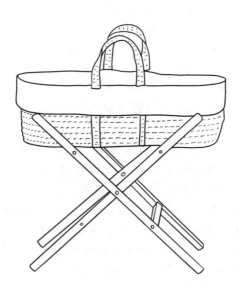

Packing your hospital bags

Whether you're planning on having your baby in hospital or not, it's recommended that from 36 weeks pregnant you have your hospital bags fully packed and ready to grab at a moment's notice to avoid a mad rush when your partner goes into labour.

These bags should contain everything that might be needed for the birth, a short stay in hospital and your baby's first few days in the world. While your partner's and baby's hospital bags are most important, don't forget to pack one for yourself too.

When the time comes, your partner will need you by her side, so it's unlikely you'll have an opportunity to nip home for a power nap, shower, shave and change of clothes. Plus, if you're the birth partner, you'll have your own essential kit that you'll need to have on you for the main event.

Her bag	Your bag	The baby's bag
Clothes to give birth in	Washbag with deodorant, toothbrush, toothpaste, razor, etc.	4 x baby vests
2 x nighties/comfortable PJs		4 x babygrows/sleepsuits
1 x cardigan	Change of clothes	2 x cotton hats
2 x nursing bras	3 x underpants	1 x cardigan
6 x pairs of big knickers	2 x pairs of socks	2 x muslins
2 x pairs of socks	Pair of sliders/flip-flops	2 x swaddles
Pair of slippers/flip-flops	Pillow from home	1 x blanket
Dressing gown	Water bottle	12 x nappies
Eye mask	Phone charger	Cotton wool
Washbag with all her home comforts and essentials		Special going home outfit
Pillow from home with 2 pillowcases	**Birth partner essentials**	
Nursing pillow	Printed copy of your birth plan	
Water bottle	Partner's maternity notes	
Phone charger	Massage oil	
Comfortable change of clothes to travel home in	Diffuser with essential oils	
Sanitary pads	Sweets and snacks	
Nipple cream	Energy drinks or isotonic gel sachets	
Reusable breast pads	Camera and charger	

Hey, Mr DJ
– creating the perfect birthing playlist

Music can play a really important role during labour in keeping your partner happy and relaxed when she needs to be while giving her a boost when she feels like she can't go on. During the third trimester, carve out some time together to discuss her favourite tunes and compile her perfect birthing playlists, which you can DJ during each stage of the birth.

If you're planning a hospital delivery, some modern birthing centres have speakers in the room which you can connect to, so be sure to ask about this at your next hospital check-up. To be on the safe side, though, always pack an alternative method to play your own music during the birth, whether from your phone with comfortable headphones, a Bluetooth speaker or via a small music player packed in your hospital bag.

Give yourself some flexibility too, creating a different playlist for each stage of labour, as your partner is likely to need different musical motivation at different times.

Early labour

To advance the progress of labour, your partner needs to avoid fear and stress as much as possible, so keep your first playlist upbeat, happy and relaxing. The aim here is to stimulate oxytocin, the hormone related to positive, happy feelings, which helps labour progress quicker. Choral music has been proven to be particularly effective, as are any songs that elicit a nostalgic, emotional response.

Active labour

Once your partner is in active labour (around 6 cm dilated and her contractions are regular, stronger and longer), the music you choose will need to work harder to keep her mind focused and relaxed. Avoid anything fast-tempo that might increase her adrenaline (which can slow and even stop the progress of labour). Calming piano music, yoga and meditation playlists or sounds of the rainforest are a safe bet.

The final push

If you're practising hypnobirthing or going into theatre for a C-section, it's best to stick with the calming tunes you chose for active labour, to maintain her focus and a peaceful birthing environment.

However, just in case it's needed, have in your back pocket a final playlist full of energizing songs that your partner loves or that send a positive message. Chances are, she will be exhausted by this stage of labour, sleep deprived and feeling like she can't go on, so your choices here can give her a boost when she needs it most.

Top 10 birthing tunes

 Now that's what I call childbirth

10. Circle of Life – Elton John

9. Let It Go – Idina Menzel

8. I Want to Break Free – Queen

7. Roar – Katy Perry

6. Don't Stop Believin' – Journey

5. Born This Way – Lady Gaga

4. Don't Stop Me Now – Queen

3. Push It – Salt-N-Pepa

2. The Final Countdown – Europe

1. I'm Coming Out – Diana Ross

Thinking about the kind of dad you want to be

Becoming a dad is a big transition. One minute you're a relatively care-free, independent guy about town... child-free, able to do whatever you like whenever you like, with your own happiness (and maybe that of your partner) your number one priority.

But as your due date approaches, something switches in your head. You're no longer just responsible for yourself and your own actions. Soon you'll have a defenceless little person in your arms who relies on you for everything. To care for them, clothe them, feed them, put a roof over their head, keep them safe and so much more. A whole raft of new responsibilities that you've never had to consider before.

This kind of newfound accountability really does make you look at things differently and think about what kind of changes you want to make for the future, not just in your own life but in the world around you too. It'll make you reconsider your priorities and what's really important. You'll start to look at your relationships, your career, your finances, your routines, and your life choices in a whole new light.

It's a major mindset shift, which all new dads go through. But the sooner you start to think about it, the easier it will be.

So, in these final weeks while you wait for your new arrival, I'd strongly encourage you to spend some time thinking about what kind of father you want to be and what kind of childhood you want your baby to have. Your answers to these two fundamental questions will give you a clear plan for what, if anything, you need to adjust while helping you make the mental transition from man to dad.

"When you have kids, you see life through different eyes."

Dave Grohl

Different types of dad

Hands-on dad

Anyone can choose to be a hands-on dad. This means knowing your stuff, doing your fair share at home and never shying away from your fatherly duties. Whether you work full-time, are only at home first thing in the morning or late at night, or only see your kid at the weekends, a hands-on dad appreciates that parenting is a partnership. No matter how tired you might be, when your partner or child needs your support, you give it willingly and without complaint, as this is the type of dad you want to be. (See page 133 for more benefits of being a hands-on dad.)

Working dad

Traditionally, the role of the father has been to provide. And, although family dynamics have changed a lot over the years, that pressure on dads to financially provide for their families has not gone away. But, while keeping a roof over your heads and food on the table is of course vital, you need to decide what is most important to you. Is it working hard to earn as much money as you can to support your family? Or could you take your foot off the gas and let your career aspirations take a backseat for a few years, freeing up time to spend with your family? (See page 132 for tips on how to juggle fatherhood and your career.)

Nostalgic vs break-the-mould dad

If you have fond memories of your own childhood, it's natural to want to give your child the same positive experiences you had growing up. In today's fast-paced world, children really do grow up so fast and don't stay wide-eyed and innocent for long. So, a nostalgic dad does everything he can to slow things down, make memories and let kids be kids for as long as possible. Of course, the exact opposite may apply if your own childhood was less than rosy – you might choose to break the mould instead, correcting past mistakes, avoiding stereotypes and taking a more modern approach to parenting.

Present dad

One of the most valuable things you can give your child is your time. When you have a busy job and bills to pay, this is easier said than done. But are there ways you can adjust your daily routine to be more present at home, supporting your partner and being there to witness your child growing up? The quality of time you give is important too and doesn't go unnoticed, so a present dad leaves his phone on the side and his worries at the door.

Eco-dad

When you become a father, it's natural to want to create a better world for your kids. But, with climate change making the future more uncertain, we all need to take some responsibility for how we live. An eco-dad knows that these changes start at home and makes the necessary adjustments to reduce his family's carbon footprint. Whether by eating less meat, driving or flying less, buying local or second-hand, or shunning disposable nappies and wipes for reusable alternatives, an eco-dad knows that every small change adds up to make a big difference. (See page 106 for everything you need to know about reusable nappies and wipes.)

Stay-at-home dad

More men today are stepping up to take on the role of stay-at-home dad. Often this is a financial decision – when your partner earns more than you, has a job that provides better benefits for your family or has less generous parental leave – and it's logical for you to take on the bulk of the childcare. Equally, you may choose to take a career break or want to try out your fathering chops full-time. This isn't the easy option... anyone who decides to do this – man or woman – deserves a huge amount of respect and appreciation. (See page 129 for more on life as a stay-at-home dad.)

Navigating the adoption process
(Tom's story)

When thinking about starting our family, we knew it was going to be adoption for us. We didn't consider any other way. It just felt right. My husband, Daniel, was 35 and had been ready for a while. I took my time getting there, but shortly before my 30th birthday we started the adoption process.

It all began with an adoption information session where prospective adopters go to their local authority or a private agency. You meet other parents who have adopted and hear first-hand accounts from social workers and people working in the sector. A lot of what you hear is quite shocking about the types of children that are placed into care and what they might have been through. Looking back, I think it was so full-on because they wanted to make sure you're serious and will stick around for the entire journey. And that we did.

After nine months of social worker meetings, training sessions, workshops and panels – which dig deep into your personal lives and often felt like therapy – we found our baby boy. Well, I say baby. He was 10 months old at the time. And it would be another agonizing four months until he would be home.

Thinking back now (eight years in), I can't quite believe we did it. We saw his profile just before Christmas and registered our interest straight away. But adoption is a tricky game. Lots of prospective adopters were interested in being his parents too. There's a lot of disappointment, and no guarantees, so you can't get your hopes up.

Within a month, we got to meet his social worker. Before she arrived at our house, I cleaned like I'd never cleaned before, baking so many brownies and cookies, all for the lovely lady to tell us that we didn't need to do any of that. She knew within the first five minutes of meeting us that it would be the perfect match.

After she left, we looked at one another like "Did that really just happen? Is he ours?"

But we couldn't accept it just yet. We needed to be approved by an adoption panel first and get through what's known as "introductions" (where you meet the foster carer and visit the baby's home, doing a little bit more for them each day to start developing a bond). None of it would feel real, though, until he was home with us.

In April, our beautiful boy, Kai, came home. At this point we were so emotionally drained. Happy drained. But drained all the same. I'll never forget the day we knocked on his foster carer's door, knowing – in that moment – our lives would never be the same again. How his little face poked around the corner of the kitchen. How he crawled right up to us. And the rest is history.

It's best to give it some time for everyone to adjust at home, before introducing friends and family. Kai took it all in his stride and made it all so easy. After a couple of weeks, our family started dropping round and the pride we felt was unmatched. Here he was. Our little boy. Our son.

As the years go by, we know we have such a responsibility to make Kai aware of his beginnings and the amazing people who got him here. We actually met his birth parents before being approved and I'm so glad we did. That we got to say "thank you" to them. We can tell Kai we met them and that means so much.

Now we have annual letter box contact (exchanging news once a year with Kai's birth parents via the adoption service) and a book of Kai's life story (which the local authority put together) with age-appropriate information, photos of his foster and birth family, ending with the story of how we became a family.

I often have to remind myself we went through this whole adoption process. With the bond we have and the love we feel, it's easy to forget. But I wouldn't have done it any other way.

Tom is an advocate for adoption and neurodivergent parenting, living in the UK with his husband Daniel and son Kai. Follow him on Instagram @unlikelydad and drop him a message if you want any advice.

Final preparations

While this chapter has covered all the big preparations you'll need to make, there are lots of other smaller (but equally important) things you can do now to make your life easier down the line.

Final checklist to tick off before your baby arrives

- If you haven't already, research what kind of parental leave and pay you are entitled to, if any, including extra leave if your baby is born prematurely. If you feel it isn't enough or fair, raise it with your boss or HR, explaining why you want, need and deserve more.

    - For added clout and security, band together with other recent or expectant parents at work and make a combined case.

    - Make sure you tell your employer early that you're expecting – around 20 weeks – so you/they can arrange proper cover for any parental leave you plan to take.

- Finalize your birth plan and have your hospital bags packed and ready to go.

- If you're planning a hospital birth, figure out how you are going to get there (drive yourself/taxi/public transport), and practise the trip a few times so you know how long it will take and what alternative routes are available if needed in a hurry.

- Organize two trusted contacts to call when you go into labour, who can look after your home/pets/house plants/other children if you suddenly need to rush to hospital in the middle of the night. Make sure they know what support you'll need and give them a key to your house too so they can do what's required and collect and deliver anything you forgot to pack.

- Think about what pain relief your partner wants to take during early labour and stock up your medicine cabinet accordingly (usually just paracetamol is recommended, though it's worth looking into buying or renting a TENS machine, which are also popular).

- Download a free contraction tracker app on your phone so you can monitor your partner's surges and know when to take her to hospital.

- Keep your phone on loud and be contactable in case your partner goes into labour.

- Let her know when you leave work each day or are ever in a position where you don't have phone signal (like going on the underground).

- Avoid booking any foreign travel, nights away or work trips that will take you more than an hour away from your partner (and risk you missing the main event!).

- Save your doctor's, midwife's and local hospital maternity ward phone numbers on your phone.

- If you have a car, install your new baby car seat and practise putting it in and out of the car. If you plan on taking a taxi to and from the hospital, practise doing this in a friend's car.

- Similarly, get to know your new pram and practise folding and unfolding it before you have to use it for real.

- Make and freeze a load of hearty meals for two that you can defrost in your early days of parenthood to save having to go shopping or cook.

- Set up an online account with your preferred supermarket and save all your favourite essential items so you can easily do your weekly shop for delivery at the click of a button.

- Finally, stock up on batteries and get yourself a mini screwdriver – lots of baby kit requires both to operate them, and you won't want to be caught short.

"BY FAILING TO PREPARE YOU ARE PREPARING TO FAIL."

Benjamin Franklin

CHAPTER 3

BEING THE BEST BIRTH PARTNER YOU CAN BE

As your due date edges closer, your partner will need your support more than ever. Her bump will be stretching her body to its limits, with a rugby ball-sized baby rearranging her internal organs and kicking her in the ribs and bladder at every opportunity. She almost certainly won't be sleeping well. Her energy levels and mobility will be at an all-time low. Her general mood may be too. Just going through her daily life will be a painful struggle; every task, a mountain to climb.

This isn't the time to book in a weekend away with your mates, stay late at work or go out for an all-nighter. In these final few days and weeks, the more available and attentive you can be towards your partner, the better it will be for everyone.

It's also likely that she (and you) will be getting increasingly anxious about the birth, especially if this is the first time for both of you. Your baby could arrive any day now and this really is the main event. When the time comes, you are going to be by her side for the entire labour and birth, front and centre, and she'll be relying on you throughout to cheer her on, keep a level head and be the best birth partner you can be.

She will be doing the hardest job of all, so think of your role as that of the support act. A small but vital part that will be remembered for years to come. The more you know what to expect, the better prepared and more useful you'll be. This chapter will help you with that.

Finally, it's important that you stay positive. During the final stages of pregnancy and the labour itself, everyone is tired and emotional. Things can get heated. But once your baby arrives and looks into your eyes for the first time, everything said or done in the heat of the moment will fade into insignificance.

Signs your partner is in labour

Leading up to your due date, your partner should have regular appointments with her midwife, who will usually let you know when your baby is "engaged" (head down into your partner's pelvis). This sometimes doesn't happen until your partner is in active labour, but it can be an early sign that the baby is getting ready to be born.

Alternatively, your baby could be "breech" (lying bottom or feet first in the uterus) which is not a safe position to be born. If so, most midwives usually wait a few days (to see if your baby gets into position on their own) or will make an appointment in hospital to physically try and turn the baby around (by pushing on your partner's bump).

Once your baby is safely engaged, it could be a matter of hours, days or even weeks before your partner goes into labour, so be on the lookout for the tell-tale signs that the process is about to begin for real:

- Her waters break (don't expect a dramatic flood of liquid like in the movies – it's usually something between a trickle and a gush. And be aware, this may not happen until much later during her labour).

- She notices any blood or spotting from her vagina.

- She sees "the show" (when the mucus plug that seals the opening of her cervix comes out of her vagina).

- Contractions or tightenings begin (remember that real contractions get more regular and stronger as they progress – see page 74).

- She has a sudden urge to go for a poo (caused by your baby's head pressing on her bowel).

If your partner experiences any of the above list, notices the baby is moving less than usual, or is worried about anything, give your midwife a call right away.

Generally, you'll be advised to stay at home until the labour progresses further, only going into hospital or sending for reinforcements for a home birth when your partner's contractions are more regular (coming consistently around three minutes apart).

What happens if your baby is late

While most babies are born before 40 weeks of gestation, it's not uncommon for some pregnancies to go on a little longer, with 42 weeks being the usual cut-off (since there is a higher risk of stillbirth after this point).

Once you pass your due date, your midwife will usually suggest a few "home remedies" in the first instance to help bring on labour. While most of these methods aren't scientifically proven to do the job, by this stage of pregnancy your partner will be willing to give anything a try to get this baby out:

Go for a long walk – to keep your partner active and let gravity do its job, helping your baby move down into position and put pressure on her cervix.

Eat spicy food – to stimulate your partner's bowel and womb.

Have unprotected sex – hopefully a pleasurable experience to help your partner release labour-inducing oxytocin. Plus, your little swimmers contain something called prostaglandins, which are thought to be able to soften the cervix.

Stimulate her nipples – just a gentle rub or massage will do to trick her body into thinking that a baby is breastfeeding from them, which can help bring on contractions.

Pregnancy massage or reflexology – a nice treat at the end of pregnancy to keep her happy, calm and relaxed, encouraging her body to release oxytocin rather than labour-delaying adrenalin.

Smell some clary sage – an essential oil that can be diluted on a handkerchief and sniffed or used in a diffuser to bring on labour (not to be used earlier in pregnancy for this reason).

If none of these approaches has the desired effect, your partner may be offered some medical intervention at around 41 weeks to kick off the labour process.

Medical interventions to get labour started

Your partner's first option is usually a membrane sweep, where a midwife or doctor puts a finger on her cervix and makes a sweeping motion to try and separate the membranes of the amniotic sac surrounding your baby, triggering labour. This can be quite uncomfortable and can cause some light bleeding, so some mums prefer to wait it out and let nature take its course.

The next option is an induction. There are two main types:

- **a chemical induction (most common) –** inserting artificial hormones into her vagina via a gel or tablet (known as a pessary, which slowly releases prostaglandins over 24 hours) or administering Syntocinon into a vein via an intravenous (IV) drip; and

- **a mechanical induction (rarely used today) –** administered via a catheter or small rods placed through her cervix, which slowly expand, stretching it open.

Neither option is pleasant, and inductions can cause labour contractions to be stronger than a natural birth, so many mothers decline the offer to have one.

Whether or not your partner accepts these interventions is entirely her choice. Just make sure you both ask your midwife or doctor about the risks and benefits of each so you can make an informed decision.

If she does go ahead with medical interventions but there's still no sign of baby emerging, it's likely that your partner will be offered a caesarean/C-section. Your baby may be getting quite large by this point, creating extra complications for a vaginal delivery, so the professionals will usually want them out as quickly and safely as possible. Again, deciding to do this is a personal choice, but it's generally recommended at this stage for the safety of both mother and baby.

Having a baby in hospital – what to expect

Every hospital maternity unit is different. While they all come with a labour ward, made up of lots of beds in one room for expectant mothers in early labour, the options for the birth itself can vary considerably.

It's only in extreme circumstances that you would deliver your baby on a ward. Most hospitals provide private rooms for the birth, which you'll be given on a first come, first served basis. Whether you get to stay in this private room after your baby is born will depend on supply and demand and may have a hefty price tag attached to it.

Alternatively, some maternity units have special midwife-led birthing centres, offering a more holistic birthing experience, including a birthing pool, sometimes an extra bed for you and a decent sound system for your birthing playlist. However, if your partner has any complications, decides she wants an epidural or needs a caesarean, it's unlikely you'll be allowed to have your baby in the birthing centre.

If you're offered the chance to visit the maternity ward in advance of the birth, take up the opportunity. It's useful to see what the options are and, importantly, know where to go when the time comes.

Other things to be aware of

- Maternity units are usually kept very warm for new mothers and babies, so don't overdress for the birth.

- With lots of new mothers in active labour, they can also get very noisy. Consider bringing noise-cancelling headphones to drown out the sounds from next door and keep your partner focused and calm.

- Your midwife will monitor baby's heart rate at intervals for reassurance, but don't expect to be monitored constantly. Depending on how many other births are in progress, you may be left alone for large chunks of time. Don't worry... your midwife will rush back anytime they're needed (though sometimes you might need to prompt them).

- It's unlikely you'll have access to drinking water in your room, so bring your own drinks to avoid having to leave your partner at key moments to rush to the nearest water fountain.

C-section – what to expect

A C-section or caesarean is an operation to deliver your baby through an incision made in your partner's tummy and womb. If one is recommended by a doctor during pregnancy due to certain medical reasons, this is referred to as a planned or elective caesarean and will usually be booked in on a specific date when your partner is around 39 weeks pregnant (earlier for twins).

The procedure may also be advised in an emergency if a vaginal birth is considered too risky. This decision could be made at any time, including in the middle of active labour, if:

- your baby is stuck in the breech position.
- your partner's labour is not progressing.
- she's experiencing excessive vaginal bleeding.
- your baby isn't getting enough oxygen and needs to be delivered immediately.

The procedure

- Be aware, it can be quite an overwhelming experience, especially in an emergency. There will be lots of medical professionals in the room, each with an important role to play.
- The whole operation normally takes under an hour to complete.
- In most cases your partner will be given a spinal or epidural anaesthetic to completely numb the lower half of her body for the procedure. She'll still be awake but won't be able to feel any pain.
- In almost all circumstances, you'll be allowed into the operating theatre with her (wearing hospital scrubs, a hat and shoe covers).
- A screen will be placed across her bump so she can't see the operation, though the doctors and nurses will let you know what's happening.
- The doctor will make a cut in her abdomen – usually about 10–20 cm long – cutting through skin, fat, fascia, abdominal muscles, peritoneum and the uterus, so your baby can be safely delivered.

- You both should be able to see and hold your baby as soon as they've been delivered, though, in an emergency, your baby may be taken straight to a paediatrician for resuscitation or a more thorough check-up. If this happens, don't panic – your baby is in the safest possible hands.

Supporting your partner after a C-section

- Be assured that a C-section is considered a quick, safe and relatively pain-free way to deliver a baby. It is however a major operation, so your partner's recovery after the birth and the level of extra support she'll need from you shouldn't be underestimated.

- Recovering from a caesarean usually takes longer than for a vaginal delivery, with mothers typically kept in hospital for longer after the birth. Keep this in mind and consider asking for some extra parental leave from work so you can be around to help.

- For up to 12 hours after the surgery, your partner will still be numb from the waist down, so you'll need to be on hand to pass her the baby and fetch her whatever she needs. Even when the anaesthetic has worn off, she'll still need your support getting dressed and going to the bathroom, so don't leave her side.

- Your partner will have multiple stitches and bandages that need changing, which will cause her discomfort, affect her mobility, and make lifting and holding the baby harder. For the first few days and weeks, she may need you to pick up, put down and bring the baby to her to speed up her recovery.

- It will be difficult for your partner to see the wound herself, so she may need you to keep an eye on it and look out for any signs of infection.

- Your partner will be advised to avoid certain activities – like driving, carrying heavy bags or anything too physical – so she will depend on you to take on more at home until she gets the all-clear at her postnatal check-up (usually after six weeks).

- The wound on her tummy will eventually form a scar, which may make her self-conscious. Be mindful of her feelings here and reassure her that you see the scar as a beautiful reminder of her strength and the amazing mother she is. If she wants to, there are specialist oils she can use on the area, once it's healed, to help the scar fade.

Home births

While most first-time parents choose to have their baby in hospital, a growing number of parents today are going back to how it used to be done and deciding to give birth in the comfort of their own home.

This approach is not recommended for anyone with existing health issues or who has experienced any complications during their pregnancy or baby loss in the past. However, it is generally considered a safe alternative to a hospital birth assuming you have the support of a specially trained home birth midwife, a safe, clean space to deliver your baby at home and easy access to a hospital (in case you need it).

Advantages of a home birth

- Antenatal appointments usually take place with your midwife at home rather than in hospital, meaning less travel and a more relaxed environment.

- You'll meet and get to know your team of midwives before the birth, providing reassurance and trust in the person who will be delivering your baby, whereas with a hospital birth there is less familiarity.

- You can more easily create your partner's perfect birthing environment for the delivery, with any home comforts she might want around her.

- Knowing that you don't have to travel to hospital and interrupt the progress of labour, home birth mothers can fully relax into the birth and focus entirely on the job at hand.

- If your partner would like a water birth, you can easily rent a birthing pool, which you inflate and fill with water yourself. In comparison, there are a limited number of birthing pools available in hospitals, so getting one isn't guaranteed.

- Even if you commit to having a home birth, you can always change your mind last minute and decide to go to hospital instead.

- After the birth, assuming all has gone to plan, your partner will be able to take a shower or bath and get into her own bed, rather than experiencing the sounds, smells and unfamiliarity of the labour ward.

Disadvantages of a home birth

- You'll have to invest time, effort and money into preparing your home for the birth.

- If your partner goes into labour before 37 weeks, she won't be allowed to have a home birth. Similarly, the longer you go past your due date, your midwife may recommend it's safer to have your baby in hospital after all.

- Pain relief options at home are usually limited to paracetamol and gas and air. If your partner thinks she might want an epidural, she'll need to have the baby in hospital.

- If your partner experiences complications during the birth, she may need to be rushed to hospital, which can create extra stress at an already stressful time while putting mother and baby at more risk.

- Equally, if your midwife has any concerns about your partner's or baby's health after the birth, you could well end up with an unplanned hospital stay.

Preparing for a home birth

- Deep clean and practise setting up your birthing area at home so you can do it quickly when the time comes.

- Collect lots of old sheets, towels and waterproof liners to protect the carpet, bed or sofa in your birthing area.

- Set up a speaker for your birthing playlist, some soft lighting and a diffuser with some nice smelling essential oils – essentially anything to create an environment that your partner finds calming.

- If you've rented a birth pool, check the contents of the box carefully on arrival, read the instructions well and do a dry run by unpacking and inflating it at least once. Also check that the hose attachments work with your home taps (though don't put any water in the rented pool until your partner's in labour).

- In the later stages of labour, put a couple of towels and your partner's dressing gown in the tumble dryer (if you have one) so they are nice and warm to wrap your new baby and partner in after the birth.

Birthing positions

If you plan on playing the role of birth partner for this special delivery, it's important that both you and your partner know the most effective birthing positions to try during labour and what to avoid.

In the heat of the moment, she may be too distracted to remember the various options or too tired to switch things up, so in many cases it will be up to you and the midwife to encourage and support her (both emotionally and physically) to try different positions throughout the birth.

If you believe everything you see in films and TV, you might think the most common birthing position is lying on a bed on your back. But, in reality, this is actually one of the least effective. During active labour, gravity is a mum's best friend as it helps to push the baby down through the birth canal towards its final destination. The more active and upright she can be, the more efficient the delivery.

Instead of lying down, most recommended positions involve a combination of standing, leaning or kneeling to help gravity do its work and to stimulate contractions. If sitting upright is comfortable, this is best done on a birthing ball rather than a static bed or chair, as the natural movement of the ball will help release tension in her hips and keep her pelvis flexible for the final stages.

During labour, new mums are also more likely to experience back pain, muscle spasms and cramp, so they are encouraged to avoid staying in the same position the whole time. By mixing things up, you can support your partner in finding the positions that are most comfortable for her while helping to manage any pain.

If you've attended your antenatal birthing classes, it's likely you will have received a leaflet with images of various birthing positions to try. I don't know about you, but I always found these unnamed positions can be a touch confusing, without any real instructions to follow. So, let's rectify that on the following pages...

The wrecking ball

A great position to maintain your partner's hip flexibility, keep her pelvis open and relax her perineum, helping reduce the risk of tearing. Help your partner sit on a birthing ball with her feet flat on the floor as she leans forward so her belly hangs between her knees. It can be quite a balancing act, though most birthing centres have support ropes hanging from the ceiling that she can hold onto. Stay close by to help her stay upright and massage her back between contractions.

The locked fridge

This position is very effective at opening your partner's pelvis wider, speeding up your baby's journey down into the birth canal. Help your partner get into a squatting position while she holds onto an open door for support. Between contractions, encourage her to sway her hips from side to side to aid flexibility and reduce the risk of leg cramps.

Three's company

Work with your midwife to help your partner into an upright kneeling position that she finds comfortable, letting her lean on you both to relieve pressure on her knees. Sharing close physical contact while offering encouraging words and maintaining eye contact should help keep your partner relaxed and her oxytocin levels up.

The citizen's arrest

During the early stages of labour, it's best for your partner to keep mobile and upright, to let gravity draw the baby down and help her cope better with each contraction. When she feels a contraction coming on, help her lean against a wall with her legs firmly planted on the ground, hip-width apart.

The water baby

If there is a birth pool available, your partner can use it throughout every stage of labour for pain relief or for the birth itself. Some hospitals will even let birth partners get into the pool at the same time (if that's something your partner wants). However, you'll generally be most useful out of the pool, holding her hand, offering words of encouragement and fetching her drinks to keep her hydrated.

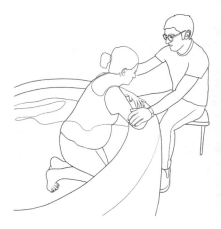

The mama dumbbell

Squats rarely top anyone's list of favourite exercises, but when it comes to giving birth, they are a great option to speed up the stages of labour. Help take your partner's weight, ensuring her knees are lower than her hips, to help your baby work their way down naturally.

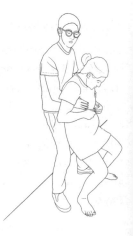

Crouching Tiger, Hidden Baby

This position is great for both mum and baby, helping open her pelvis, taking pressure off her spine to ease back pain, while boosting your baby's oxygen levels during labour. To get into this position, help your partner kneel forward over a pile of pillows on the bed (alternatively a beanbag or birthing ball on the floor), with her knees apart and bottom below her belly.

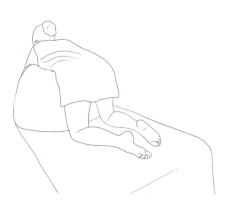

The Zoolander

If your partner suffers from back-ache during labour, slightly squatting while leaning with her back against a wall can help relieve this pain, making her contractions a bit more manageable. Some new mums also don't like physical touch during labour, so this position is a good upright option to try, as it uses the wall for support (rather than you).

What to expect during the birth

The first stage

The first stage of birth is by far the longest and usually lasts for hours (though it can be days). It begins from the first early signs of labour (covered on page 62) and finishes when your partner's cervix has dilated to around 10 cm and your baby is ready to be born.

During this first stage, your partner will experience contractions or surges, which are literally her cervix contracting to push the baby towards and through the birth canal. These will come in waves, usually lasting around one minute, starting small and building to a climax before falling away again. In early labour, these surges will be irregular and uncomfortable but, on the whole, manageable. As things progress, they will intensify, become more regular and get increasingly painful for your partner, so she'll need your support more and more as this first stage progresses.

Pain relief

Your partner can have paracetamol and may be offered gas and air to help relieve the pain (administered via a special mouthpiece which she holds and breathes through when needed). Some mothers find this really helps, though it can cause nausea, so it isn't for everyone.

If your partner wants something stronger, she may be able to have a pethidine or diamorphine injection in her thigh or buttock. This can take up to 20 minutes to work so isn't recommended in the later stages of labour as it can make your baby sleepy.

The most effective natural pain relief method is getting into a birth pool, as the soothing water (kept at body temperature) can aid relaxation and pain management while giving a mother the feeling of weightlessness. If a pool is available, your partner can sit or kneel in it at any stage and, if she wants to and there are no complications, she can even give birth in the pool (known as a water birth).

Finally, your partner may want to ask for an epidural – an injection of anaesthetic into her spine – which numbs her body from the waist down, making the rest of the birth relatively pain-free.

But be aware...

- there are side effects and some potential risks involved (your doctor will explain these to you).

- it isn't always possible to have one (for example, if labour is too far progressed).

- your partner can't use the birthing pool after having an epidural.

- your baby's heart rate will be continuously monitored using a cardiotocograph (CTG) via an elastic belt strapped around your partner's abdomen.

- an epidural increases the probability that your partner will need an instrumental delivery.

- it can significantly slow down the whole birthing process, meaning your partner may be in labour for many more hours than if she'd skipped it.

What you can do to help

- Be by her side for every contraction, to offer support, a word of encouragement or your hand to squeeze.

- Massage her lower back in between and during each contraction, as back-aches are likely.

- Have a sick bowl ready, as it's common for mothers to vomit during this stage of labour.

- Encourage her to rest as much as possible between surges, as you won't know how long this stage will last.

- Offer her snacks and drinks to build up her energy reserves.

- Run her a warm bath to help her stay as relaxed as possible.

- Encourage her to go to the toilet regularly and have a poo if she can, as this will free up space and relieve pressure on her internal organs.

- Help her to move around between contractions and suggest alternative birthing positions if she's feeling stiff, uncomfortable or has been using the same one for a while.

The second stage

This stage begins when your partner is fully dilated and your baby is ready to be born. There's no doubt that this is the most intense part of the birth. It's likely that you will both be exhausted and your partner's worries about giving birth will be reaching boiling point.

At this point, your partner's contractions will be coming thick and fast – lasting longer and feeling stronger than any time during the first stage, with a break of just a minute or two before the next one starts.

If she hasn't had an epidural, you may notice her start to shake or get louder, with some mothers making a groaning or huffing sound, which can be an indication that she's ready to start pushing. It's likely she will be feeling especially nauseous, so she may well vomit if she hasn't already. The biggest sign of all is your partner saying she can feel increased pressure in her bottom and an uncontrollable urge to push. Just before the baby's head is ready to be born, she'll feel an intense stinging around the opening of her vagina too (often referred to as "the ring of fire").

What you can do to help

- Stay by your partner's side, but try not to get in the way – let the doctor or midwife do their job and let them guide her through the pushing stage.
- Have a sick bowl and bottle of water or isotonic drink ready in case she needs it.
- If your partner is feeling hot, dab a cold flannel on her forehead, cheeks and neck.
- Reassure her that she's amazing, doing so well and that you love her.
- Above all else, stay positive and keep your focus on your partner at all times.

The third stage

She's done it! Your baby is born and you're now proud parents. But it isn't over yet.

First you need to cut the cord, a job us dads usually have the honour of doing. If you've decided in your birth plan to delay the cord clamping and "wait for white", it usually takes between one and five minutes for the blood to flow through the cord before the midwife clamps it and passes you the scissors. Just be aware that if there are any concerns for the mother or baby, for example, if your baby is struggling to breathe or the cord is wrapped around their neck, the midwife will usually clamp and cut the cord quickly to get to work on your baby.

Within moments, you and your partner will have your baby in your arms, cleaned up and wrapped in a warm towel ready for their first try of breastfeeding. But it doesn't end there. Your partner still has one more important job to do... delivering the placenta and membranes (sometimes referred to as the "afterbirth").

Although it's the last thing she'll want to do at this moment, it's important to get the placenta out safely and in one piece. If it breaks or any of the placenta membranes are left inside, this can require surgery or cause severe afterpains for your partner.

Your partner's contractions will continue after the birth as her womb works to push out the placenta, though these are generally milder than during active labour. If she chooses to "birth the placenta" naturally (physiological management – see page 37 for a reminder), this process can take up to an hour. Whereas if your partner chooses active management, she'll be given an injection in her thigh and the placenta should come out in less than 30 minutes. Usually, the midwife will gently pull on the cord to deliver it, asking your partner to help by gently pushing.

There's a chance that your partner may experience a tear during the second stage of labour – a literal tearing of her perineum, the area between the vagina and anus – during the birth. This could be intentional if the doctor had to make a small incision (episiotomy) to help the baby come out or a natural side effect of the birth.

There are various degrees of tear to be aware of:

- First-degree – small and skin deep, usually left to heal by itself
- Second-degree – deeper tears into the muscle of the perineum that usually require stitches (generally done then and there in the room)
- Third-degree – a tear that cuts into the muscle that controls the anus, which requires surgery to correct
- Fourth-degree – a tear that extends even further into the lining of the anus, requiring surgery

Keep these in mind after the birth as the type of tear your partner has will affect her recovery time and the type of additional support and reassurance she'll need from you.

What you can do to help

- As tempting as it can be to focus on the baby right now, don't forget that your partner is in pain and in a vulnerable position, so she will need your continued attention and support.
- Make sure your partner has the first hold of the baby and wait until you're offered your chance. After what your partner has just done, it's only right she should get the first cuddle.
- Don't forget to take lots of photos of mum and baby during this first proper meeting – they are pictures you'll treasure for years to come.
- Keep a mental note of everything the doctors and nurses are saying after your baby is born – in the coming days it's likely your partner will want to relive every detail of the birth and she'll expect you to remember.
- If your partner has a third or fourth-degree tear, she will be whisked off to theatre to fix it (alone) while you are left holding the baby. Send her off with a kiss and reassuring word, as the thought of leaving her baby so soon will be a heart-wrencher.

Questions to ask if things don't go to plan

Every birth experience is unique and rarely goes exactly to plan. There are always twists and turns, unexpected surprises and decisions to be made, especially if this is your partner's first baby. So, while you should go into it with the best intentions of following your birth plan to a tee, be prepared that there's likely to be at least one moment where you'll have to change course or compromise.

Should this happen, usually instigated by a concern that the birth may not be progressing as it should, your doctor or midwife will recommend an alternative course of action for the safety of mum and baby. Whether or not you follow their recommendation is entirely up to you and your partner, so don't feel pressured to make a decision straight away without all the facts.

While the medical advice is very likely to be sound, that doesn't mean it's compulsory or the only solution. There may be an alternative that is closer to what your partner wants, that doesn't involve medical intervention or that avoids unnecessary pain or risks.

But the only way you'll know that is if you ask. So, before compromising on your birth plan, make it your role as the birth partner to ask the professionals in the room your "BRAIN" questions:

Benefits – What are the benefits of this course of action?

Risks – What are the risks to mother and baby if we do this? Ask for percentages so you can assess the risks properly.

Alternatives – What are the alternatives? Is there another way?

Instincts – Ask your partner, "What do your instincts tell you?"

Nothing – What if we do nothing? For five minutes, 30 minutes or longer? Can we wait and see what happens before committing to this?

By asking these questions, you and your partner can be as informed as possible before making any decision, safe in the knowledge that you understand the risks and rationale of what is being suggested.

Meeting your baby for the first time

There's no experience more special in your life than meeting your new baby for the first time. You've been waiting for this moment for so long, and it really does live up to the hype.

When you first see your baby emerge, don't be surprised if they are almost purple in colour. This is the result of minor oxygen deprivation in the last moments of birth, but they should develop a more normal skin tone once they've taken their first few breaths.

It's likely that your baby will be born with a white, creamy substance all over them – known as vernix caseosa – which is also entirely normal. This coating covers the foetus during the third trimester and helps their skin adapt to life on the outside, acting as a natural moisturizer and protecting them from infection. The earlier your baby is born, the more of this substance they're likely to have on them.

While it can be tempting to wipe this vernix off, it's recommended that you leave it on their skin for between six to 24 hours, and it should slowly absorb naturally.

When it's your turn to hold the baby, make sure you give your hands a thorough wash first and remember to support your baby's head – best done with one hand cupping the back of their head and the other supporting their back and bottom.

To help create an immediate bond with the baby, new mums are encouraged to try skin-to-skin, where your naked baby is placed directly on her bare chest (with a towel or blanket on top for warmth). This not only builds connection but also helps regulate your baby's temperature and heartbeat after the birth.

This same concept is also recommended for dads. So, when it's your turn to hold the baby, don't be embarrassed to whip off your top and give it a try. If you're too self-conscious to go topless with so many nurses in the room, try to remember to wear a shirt for the birth which you can unbutton to get your own skin-to-skin moment with your baby. You won't regret it.

"NEVER IS A MAN MORE OF A MAN THAN WHEN HE IS THE FATHER OF A NEWBORN."

Matthew McConaughey

CHAPTER 4

LIFE WITH A NEWBORN

This is it. The moment you've been waiting for. Your beautiful baby has arrived and you're now officially a dad. Shit has very much just got real. So now what?

If you had your baby in hospital, like most parents do for their first, you're in a safe space. You're surrounded by doctors and nurses who have seen it all a thousand times before, checking in on you regularly to make sure mum and baby are healthy and happy. This brief moment is one to treasure.

It's a time you'll never get back, so try to make the most of it. Ask lots of questions, soak up every piece of advice from the experts in the room, take loads of photos and catch up on some sleep if you can. But mostly, just try to enjoy this special moment with your newborn while you have so much support on tap. Because soon, you'll be discharged and allowed to go home, let loose into the world, as your new family unit, to fend for yourselves.

In this chapter, I'll give you everything you need to know about the next few weeks and months as a new dad, from the basics of how to hold your baby, change a nappy and put them down to sleep to more advanced topics like how you can support your partner's recovery, bond with your baby, smash parental leave and control the crowds of well-wishers desperate to meet your new arrival in the flesh.

It's going to be an unforgettable time of your life, full of ups and downs, moments of pure joy and pure terror, with touches of sleep deprivation, anxiety and confusion thrown in for good measure. But believe me, over the months ahead, every time you smell your baby's head, every time their tiny hand grabs your finger, and every time they stop crying and fall asleep in the safety of your arms, you'll feel love like you've never experienced before and will never want this time to end.

Hospital stays and premature arrivals

If mum and baby are well and your midwife has no concerns, you'll usually be given the all-clear to go home between six and 24 hours after the birth.

However, there are various reasons why you might be encouraged to stay in hospital a little longer, including if:

- your partner had an emergency C-section or experienced complications during the birth.
- your partner had surgery for a third- or fourth-degree tear.
- your baby has any underlying health concerns.
- your baby isn't feeding.
- your baby was born prematurely and needs extra monitoring or support.

These are not necessarily things to worry about. If the professionals have any concerns, they would rather be safe than sorry, wanting you nearby so that they can give you the extra support you need while ruling out anything worrying.

For most new parents, this could mean a few extra days in hospital, but if your baby has any underlying health issues or was born prematurely, your stay could be longer (see page 87).

Regular check-ups

During the first day of your baby's life, your midwife will monitor mum and baby closely. Among other things, they will make sure you are comfortable feeding, changing and cleaning your baby (being especially careful of their sensitive umbilical cord stump) while also looking out for:

- any immediate health concerns (including the presence of jaundice, any infection of the umbilical cord or eyes, or thrush in the mouth);
- how well your baby is feeding and latching (including looking out for tongue-tie – see page 147);
- whether your baby is gaining weight; and
- how your partner is coping, both physically and mentally.

What is jaundice?

Jaundice is a very common condition in newborn babies, caused by a natural build-up of a yellow substance called bilirubin in their blood, which gives their skin an obvious yellow tint. Around six in every ten babies develop jaundice, and it is even more common for babies born prematurely.

Most babies with jaundice don't need any treatment as the symptoms usually pass within two weeks. Giving your baby fresh air and exposing them to natural light helps speed this process along, while good feeders are best at "passing" bilirubin through their system when they pee.

However, if tests show very high levels of bilirubin in your baby's blood, you may be kept in the hospital for longer, either for monitoring or proactive treatment.

First feeds

If your partner has chosen to breastfeed, one of the first things your baby will do after they're born is be put on your partner's chest for their first try at breastfeeding. Though this first attempt isn't always successful, from that moment on, your partner will become something of a feeding machine.

It's advised during the first 24 hours (and for many weeks to come) that you feed your baby on demand, otherwise known as "responsive feeding". To begin with, this could be as often as once every hour, though this militant schedule should ease before too long.

For these early feeds, your midwife will coach your partner through each one, showing her what to do and how best to hold the baby while helping your baby get a good latch onto the breast.

For a new mum who has never breastfed before, this can be a painful, often frustrating and emotionally draining exercise, which is anything but simple to get right. Make sure you pay close attention to the midwife's advice here, so that you can help your partner recall all the technical details and suggest different things to try if something isn't working when you get home.

In the first few days after the birth, your baby won't be drinking breast milk as you might imagine it. Initially, your partner's breasts produce something called colostrum instead, a thick, golden-yellow liquid packed with exactly what your baby needs to start growing.

While your baby will feed regularly, they'll only need a tiny amount of colostrum at each feed – about a teaspoon's worth – which is plenty, given your baby's stomach will be no larger than a standard marble at this point.

If your baby is not taking to breastfeeding yet, your partner may be advised to massage her breasts to release colostrum, which can be collected in a tiny syringe and fed to your baby that way, either by you or your partner.

The more your baby breastfeeds, the more their sucking action will stimulate your partner's milk supply, meaning she produces more. And within a few days, her milk will start to "come in", with her breasts growing in size as they start to produce real breast milk.

DADVICE

While most dads enjoy this development, it's best to admire from afar – look, don't touch – as the non-stop feeding routine will make her breasts sore and her nipples extremely sensitive (possibly even cracked and bleeding). Concentrate instead on keeping your partner well hydrated and her breastfeeding snack basket full (see page 138).

Feeding your baby will take up such a huge part of your new parenting life that it warrants its own chapter. Jump forward to Chapter 5 for the full lowdown on breast and bottle feeding, plus how you can be most helpful here.

What to expect if your baby is born prematurely

If your baby is born before 37 weeks pregnant, they'll be considered premature. If we're talking just a few days or a week before this milestone, so long as they are a healthy weight and the midwives are happy, they should need minimal intervention. But the earlier they're born, the more intensive the treatment they'll need and the longer you'll need to stay in hospital.

Premature babies are usually born smaller, with less body fat, often with fine hair covering most of their body (this normally falls out in the final stages of pregnancy). As they aren't yet "fully cooked", their organs may still need time to develop, so they may require extra help with breathing, feeding or controlling their body temperature.

If so, you'll either be placed in a dedicated nursery unit with specialist nurses trained to help preterm babies, or (if more intensive care is needed) they might need to spend some time in a neonatal intensive care unit (NICU) where they can be monitored day and night.

In NICU, premature babies are usually kept in an incubator, a kind of enclosed plastic bassinet, which keeps them safe and warm. It's likely they'll have various sensors taped to their body to monitor their vital signs and have breathing and feeding tubes connected to them. As scary as this can be, just remember that they are in the best possible place, receiving the best possible care.

How long you stay in NICU will depend on how your baby responds to the treatment. But generally, they stay in hospital until around when their due date should have been or once they can breathe without any support, are feeding well and gaining weight, have a stable body temperature and are free from any major health concerns.

DID YOU KNOW?

Being born early won't necessarily hamper your baby's future potential. Some of history's most acclaimed people were born prematurely, including Albert Einstein, Sir Isaac Newton, prima ballerina Anna Pavlova, Stevie Wonder and Sir Winston Churchill!

Bonding with your baby while they're incubated

This can be torture for new parents... when all you want to do is hold your baby, but the only real contact you can have is putting your hand through a hole in the side of the incubator. As difficult as this situation can be, don't lose heart. There are still things you can do to build a bond with your baby and be a part of their care:

- Stay with them as much as you can, taking every opportunity for physical contact that the NICU nurses allow. Gently resting your hand on their head or stroking their hand can be so beneficial for both you and your baby, even if you can't hold them. When your baby's up to it, the nurses should give you a chance to hold them for some special skin-to-skin time too.

- Though it will be hard to tear yourself away, both you and your partner need to get some sleep, so suggest taking the night-times in shifts.

- Your baby can still hear you, so make every effort to talk, read or sing to them so they learn to recognize your voice.

- Ask to help the nurses with your baby's daily care, from cleaning them and changing their nappy to helping with their feeds, even if only through a feeding tube. The more involved you are in their care, the closer bond you'll be able to create.

- Don't suffer in silence. If there are any questions you have, or anything you don't understand, ask the doctors and nurses to explain what's going on.

- And, as tempting as it might be to "stay strong", don't be afraid to show your emotions. It will be a comfort to your partner to know you are feeling the same things that she is.

Going home and settling into family life

As you walk through your front door, babe in arms, don't be surprised to feel a massive sense of relief, tinged with a healthy dose of fear. This is it now – your new life as parents – and it's up to you to keep this little person alive and well. It's a lot of pressure on your shoulders, and there's a huge amount to figure out. But first...

- Take a moment to relax and enjoy the moment. Make yourselves a drink, have a seat and recount the crazy experience you've both just been through.

- If you had to rush to hospital in the throes of labour, it's likely that parts of your home will still be in disarray. While your partner chills with the baby, have a quick whip around to make the bed, wash the dishes and have a general tidy up.

- You'll probably need to put the baby down at some point soon for a nap, so get their Moses basket and changing station set up if it isn't already.

- After spending however many hours or days in hospital, both you and your partner will want to have a proper wash and change your clothes. Run your partner a hot bath or shower and let her have first dibs while you get some quality one-on-one time with your new pride and joy.

- You'll both almost certainly be exhausted and will need to get some rest, so as soon as your baby is napping, head straight to bed. Don't worry if it's the middle of the day. Just try to get some shut-eye while you have the chance.

- Take it slow, and don't feel any pressure to hit the phones to tell people your news or accept requests to visit you and the new baby – this can all wait. This time is precious and it's just for you.

Finding your feet

From this point onwards, the next few weeks can become a bit of a blur. Most newborn babies will usually sleep a lot during their first week – around 16 hours a day, in short bursts. Take every opportunity you can to rest and recover, as these brief moments of calm won't last for long.

At the beginning, your baby will feed between eight and 15 times a day, throughout the day and night. This will put a lot of pressure on your partner, especially if she's breastfeeding, as breastfed babies usually feed more often than bottle and formula-fed ones. Try to take some of the pressure off by shouldering most of the household chores and non-feeding baby duties yourself, so your partner can focus her attention on feeding the baby, her own recovery and getting some rest in between feeds.

If you decide to bottle feed your baby, it's recommended that you offer them 30–60 ml (1–2 ounces) of expressed breast milk or first infant formula on demand, usually every couple of hours. In this instance, you can take on more of the feeding responsibilities yourself, to give your partner a chance to rest and recover.

With your baby feeding so often, all that liquid needs to go somewhere, so expect to change as many nappies every day as your baby has feeds. In the beginning, this will mainly be wet nappies rather than pooey ones, as it can take a few days for a newborn to have their first poo (head to page 105 for the lowdown on newborn poos to avoid a nasty shock when they arrive).

The more nappy changes you can do, the more rest your partner will be able to get in between feeds. Your help will be most useful during the night, so take one for the team and drag yourself out of bed to change and settle the baby after every night feed.

While the regularity of feeds and nappy changes should ease off after a couple of weeks, reducing to six to eight times a day, don't underestimate the toll this new routine will take on you and your partner. It can take a while to get into the swing of things, so don't expect an easy ride.

DID YOU KNOW?

It's very common for babies to lose weight in their first few days after birth. If your baby is being breastfed, you can expect them to lose between 5% and 7% of their birth weight during the first four days, before they start putting on weight again. For bottle-fed babies, you have more control over how much they are drinking so the weight loss is generally a bit less.

All being well, your baby should have got back to their birth weight by around day 14. If not, or their weight loss is greater than the percentages above, your midwife or health visitor will recommend a strict feeding plan to ensure your baby is getting enough.

Health checks

Until your baby is back up to their birth weight, you can expect regular appointments with a health visitor to check how you are all getting along. These could be home visits, or you might be asked to travel to your nearest health centre. Either way, try to attend as many of these appointments as you can, as they are great sources of information and reassurance, especially if you're struggling with anything.

During these visits, the health visitor will always weigh your baby to monitor their weight gain or loss. This can be quite stressful as your baby needs to be stripped naked before getting on the scales, which usually ends in tears, so try to be on hand for emotional support.

The health visitor will also ask questions to assess your partner's emotional well-being, to make sure she's coping with her new parenting responsibilities. In particular, they want to check that every new mum has support in these early weeks, especially during the onset of the "baby blues". These usually hit during the first week after childbirth, causing mothers to experience a low mood and feel depressed due to hormonal imbalances and lack of sleep. Head to page 120 for more on how you can support here.

Blood spot test

Between five and eight days after the birth, your midwife should offer a heel prick test (or blood spot test) for your baby, taking a tiny drop of blood from your baby's heel to test for rare but serious health conditions, including cystic fibrosis and sickle cell disease.

Hearing screening test

Within the first few weeks of your baby's life, you should be offered a newborn hearing screening test. This test involves putting a small earpiece into your baby's ear and playing some gentle clicking sounds before checking for any physical response from your baby. The test only lasts a few minutes, normally causes no distress and you should be given your results straight away.

Sometimes babies don't respond to this test, for example, if they are distracted or unsettled. Don't worry – this doesn't necessarily mean they have any hearing impairment or deafness, though they will need some additional testing just to make sure. This usually involves a slightly longer test, in which the specialist will place three small sensors on your baby's head and neck before playing more clicking sounds with the aid of some soft headphones over their ears.

If there is still no response, you will be booked in for a longer test (one to two hours) with a hearing specialist at an audiology clinic. They will be able to confirm if your baby does have any hearing issues and, if so, put a plan in place to support you all through it.

Vaccinations

Whether or not your baby has vaccinations is the parents' personal choice, though they are highly recommended, both to protect your own baby and also to prevent the spread of diseases that could harm any other babies you come into contact with.

Generally, you will be offered the first round of vaccinations when your baby is eight weeks old, with second and/or third doses of each vaccine given at 12 weeks and 16 weeks. After that, the next recommended vaccinations won't be needed until your baby is one.

Get these, and your baby will be protected from a long list of serious, potentially life-threatening diseases including meningitis, diphtheria, hepatitis B, polio, tetanus, whooping cough, measles, mumps and rubella, to name just a few.

DADVICE

Ask your doctor or nurse about how best to deal with any side effects of the vaccinations, should they arise. Some can cause your baby to develop a fever, which can be easily managed by giving them liquid paracetamol straight after the injection (but this isn't recommended for every vaccination). Try to attend the appointment, too, as it's quite a big deal for everyone involved, and be careful not to knock or put any pressure on the area where your baby had the injection, as it can be quite tender.

TOP TIP

If your baby rejects a syringe of medicine, try putting a bottle teat over the end of the syringe before slowly squirting the medicine through that. Most babies will instinctively suck on the teat, making the whole process easier while avoiding wasted medicine or spills.

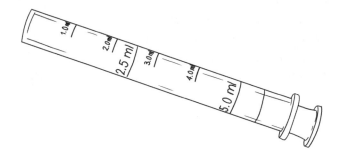

DID YOU KNOW?

Five crazy facts about newborn babies

1. **Newborn babies are crazily strong**
   So strong, in fact, that if a newborn baby was to grip a washing line with its tiny little hands, its whole body would hang suspended in mid-air (as babies' bent fingers have evolved to be powerful enough to support their entire weight). Whatever you do, though, please do not (I repeat, DO NOT) try this at home.

2. **Newborn babies can't cry**
   Howl, yes. Scream, definitely. But cry? No! Babies' tear ducts don't actually develop fully until they're around three weeks old, so it can take up to four or five months until some babies' first tear will drop.

3. **Babies are programmed to react to smiling faces from birth**
   Extensive research has shown that newborn babies prefer looking at a drawing of a face rather than a random pattern and that they prefer smiling faces to grumpy ones!

4. **Unlike adults, babies can breathe and swallow at the same time**
   It's true. Up until around the seven-month mark, babies can indeed swallow and breathe simultaneously, which explains how they can go to town on a boob or bottle for so long without coming up for air. However, snotty noses are a baby's kryptonite, blocking this superpower (albeit temporarily).

5. **Newborn babies grow insanely fast**
   So quickly, in fact, that if an average 3.6-kg (8-lb) baby were to continue growing at the same rate as they do during their first year of life, by the time they reached their 20th birthday, they'd be more than 7 m (25 ft) tall and weigh a whopping 143 kilograms (that's 22 ½ stone)!

Sleeping arrangements

How long, how often and how well your baby sleeps is every new parent's obsession. Sleep is crucial to a baby's development, but it also has a massive impact on your life too. Their sleep patterns dictate how much you can get done in a day, how much sleep you manage to get yourself and consequently your general mood and ability to cope with everyday life.

It truly is one of the hardest things to navigate during early parenthood, a rite of passage that every new parent has to go through (but ultimately survives).

While it may be tempting to try and establish a sleep routine for your baby right from the outset, hold off. Their little minds are too small right now to comprehend any kind of routine, so for the time being you'll need to go with the flow and follow their lead. At the beginning, your baby's safety and comfort are most important, so make them your top priority.

Jump forward to Chapter 6 for everything you need to know about newborn sleeping patterns and establishing a routine.

Creating a comfortable and safe sleeping space

Newborn babies spend the majority of their day asleep, so the spaces you create for them to have their naps are hugely important. Most new parents put their baby down in a Moses basket, bassinet or crib for the majority of their sleeps during the day, though it's totally fine to do some naps in a pram, in your arms or in a baby sling or carrier (highly recommended for naps on the go, or when you're too tired to hold them/ need to be hands-free).

During the night, it's recommended that babies sleep in the same room as their parents for the first six months of their life before moving into their own room (if you have one) from that point onwards. This is to reduce the risk of sudden infant death syndrome (SIDS) – the sudden and unexpected death of a baby where no cause is found – which is the principal concern behind almost every piece of sleeping advice.

To minimize the risk of SIDS:

- Always put your baby to sleep on their back. Once they are strong enough to roll onto their side or stomach, usually around six months, it's okay to let them stay in this position to sleep, but still always start them off on their back.

- Keep their sleep space clear (with no cuddly toys, pillows, sleep positioners or wedges) and ensure their mattress is firm and new.

- Be cautious of overheating. The room where your baby sleeps should be between 16 and 20°C (60 and 68°F), while you will also need to ensure they have the right amount of clothing/bedding layers to stay warm (see page 171). And always keep your baby's bed away from radiators and out of direct sunlight.

- If using a blanket, position your baby with their feet at the end of the Moses basket or cot, with the blanket tucked in firmly on all three sides, making sure it doesn't come up above shoulder height. Even the youngest babies can wriggle down underneath the blanket, where they are at risk of overheating.

- Keep any wires or cables (e.g. phone chargers or curtain cords) well away from their sleeping space.

- If you have pets at home that could jump into the crib, don't leave your sleeping baby unattended. Look into buying a special cat net, which goes over the crib, if this does emerge as a problem.

- Co-sleeping (sleeping with your baby in your bed) is not recommended by most healthcare professionals as it increases the risk of SIDS.

DADVICE

Always look up the most recent public health recommendations for safe sleeping, as these do evolve as new research is published. On that note, be especially wary of conflicting or outdated advice from friends and older relatives, as the sleeping positions considered safest today are quite different to what was the norm when we were kids.

The great co-sleeping debate

Despite the risks, co-sleeping is still common and fans of the practice wouldn't have it any other way. They argue that:

- it can help your baby feel safer and more secure, building a closer bond for mum and baby.
- it helps breastfeeding mothers get more rest during the night, as they are able to feed right there and then without needing to get up and out of bed.
- it can help babies sleep and settle better during the night, as they can be calmed as soon as they start to stir or grumble.

If you and your partner do decide to co-sleep with your baby, here are some tips to do it as safely as possible:

- Ensure your mattress is firm and flat. You shouldn't co-sleep if your mattress is too soft, dipped, memory foam or a waterbed.
- Make sure your baby has their own clear sleep space on the bed, removing any of your pillows and covers that could end up on or around your baby.
- Lie your baby flat on the mattress – on their back – without a pillow or covers, and swaddle or use a baby sleeping bag to ensure they stay warm during the night.
- Ensure your baby is well away from the edge of the bed in case they could fall out or get stuck down the side if your bed is against a wall.
- Don't let pets or other children sleep in your bed at the same time.

And importantly, never share a bed with your baby if:

- they were born prematurely before 37 weeks or had a birth weight of less than 2.5 kg (5.5 lb).
- you are a smoker.
- you've had an alcoholic drink that evening or taken any prescription or recreational drugs that could make you drowsy.

How to swaddle your baby

Swaddling is an age-old technique that parents have been doing for thousands of years. It involves wrapping your newborn baby up in a light, breathable blanket to keep them safe, warm and contained while sleeping.

Lots of parents swear by it, as swaddling is thought to mimic the snug environment your baby enjoyed in the womb, aiding better and longer sleep while preventing a newborn's "startle reflex" (when they wake themselves up with an involuntary jolt of their arms or legs as they drift off).

It's quick and easy to do using a large muslin or cellular blanket, or you can buy ready-made swaddle wraps. Though swaddling recommendations vary country by country, it's generally accepted that you can swaddle a newborn baby with their arms inside when they are too small to roll over. But when they start showing signs of rolling, they should only be swaddled from below their armpits, so their arms are free to move.

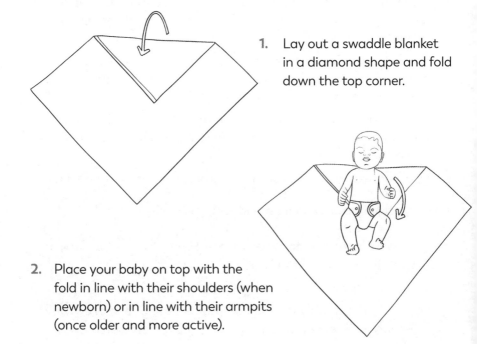

1. Lay out a swaddle blanket in a diamond shape and fold down the top corner.

2. Place your baby on top with the fold in line with their shoulders (when newborn) or in line with their armpits (once older and more active).

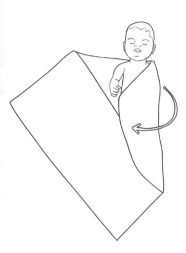

3. Fold the right flap of the blanket over your baby, tucking it firmly under their left side.

4. Fold the bottom flap up, ensuring their feet are properly contained.

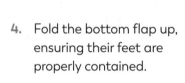

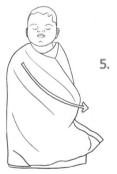

5. Fold the left flap over, tucking it under their right side, ensuring there isn't any loose fabric near your baby's face.

6. Check your baby is neatly contained, but allow some flexibility so they can move their legs and arms freely.

How to pick up and hold your baby

Picking up a tiny newborn baby is always nerve-wracking, but you'll get used to it in no time. As gentle as you need to be, they aren't made of glass, so a firm, secure grip is key.

The main thing to remember when picking up and holding your baby is to always support their head and neck. They won't develop neck strength and head control until they are around three to four months old, so this is essential to prevent injury should their head flop by accident.

Picking up your baby

Put one hand under your baby's neck, stretching out your fingers to support the back of their head, neck and shoulders. Then, slide your other hand underneath their bottom on their alternate side, before leaning completely into your baby and lifting them carefully up into your body. While still supporting their head and neck, you can then manoeuvre them into different positions easily.

Different ways to hold your baby

There are lots of different holds you can try, but generally they fall into the following six variations, which all provide the necessary head and neck support your baby needs (while also being comfortable for you).

- To get your baby to sleep, the shoulder, football and belly holds are your best options.

- When bottle-feeding your baby, sit down and use the football or lap hold. For breastfeeding, there are a whole host of other positions your partner can try (see page 141).

- For burping your baby after a feed, try the shoulder and belly holds (the latter being especially beneficial for babies with colic (see page 144), so you can massage their back at the same time).

- To interact and bond with your baby, the lap and face-to-face holds are ideal so you can maintain eye contact.

- The chair hold is great for showing your baby the world around them while also being one of the most comfortable for you to maintain.

Shoulder hold

Football hold

Belly hold

Lap hold

Face-to-face hold

Chair hold

How to burp your baby

Burping (or winding) is a fundamental skill all new parents need to learn. When your baby feeds, with each gulp of milk they drink they can also take in some air (particularly if they haven't latched onto the breast or bottle properly). This leads to trapped wind, which can be very uncomfortable and cause your baby to cry, throw up, struggle to sleep or wake up prematurely.

To avoid this, burp your baby after every feed (and don't give up too quickly if you don't hear immediate results). As a general rule, you should try winding them for up to five minutes at a time, or until you get a couple of good burps out. Some babies like a burp mid-feed too, so look out for signs of trapped wind while feeding (for example, pulling faces, arching their back, refusing to feed), and give burping a go before resuming.

Best burping positions

Shoulder burp – Hold your baby upright with their chin resting on your shoulder, then gently pat and rub their back. The aim is to encourage excess air up and out, so start from the bottom of their back and work your way up, making sure to pat both sides of their spine. When rubbing, a circular or up-and-down motion is best. Walking around or gently bouncing can help too.

Lap burp – Sit your baby on your lap facing away from you, supporting their chest with your palm while using your thumb and index finger to gently hold their chin and jaw. Lean them forward slightly and pat or rub their back until they burp.

Lying down burp – Lie your baby face down across your lap, lifting one of your legs up slightly so that your baby's head is higher than their chest. Support their chin with one hand (being careful not to put any pressure on their throat) and repeat the usual patting and rubbing motion.

> **TOP TIP**
>
> Make sure you always have a muslin over your shoulder or under your baby's chin to catch any milk that might "resurface" during the process.

Nappy changing 101

It's a dirty job, but somebody's got to do it. Over the next few years, you're going to change potentially thousands of nappies, so let's kick off the process with a quick how-to guide. While nappy changing will soon become a core life skill, which you'll be able to do in the dark, under extreme time pressure and with one arm tied behind your back, it does take some practice to nail it.

Getting your set-up right

First things first, set up your main changing area at home, which includes:

- A changing table – either purpose-made or a piece of furniture that is the correct height (just above your waist, ideally, to save your back when bending over to change nappies multiple times per day).

- A changing mat – a padded or foam mattress with a waterproof cover, a separate removable cotton cover and a hand towel for your baby to lie on (and to catch any leaks).

- Plenty of clean nappies – size newborn and size one at the start. Be mindful that you could get through around ten a day during the first few weeks with a new baby.

- Cotton wool and a bowl of water to clean your baby's bum (recommended instead of wipes when they're newborn).

- Nappy cream – apply lightly to minimize and soothe nappy rash.

- Poo bags and an airtight nappy bin (if you're using disposables) for soiled nappies to avoid stinking out your home. Not essential right away as newborn baby poo doesn't really smell.

DADVICE

Wherever possible, use your main changing table when on nappy duty. While changing a nappy on the bed, floor or sofa might seem like a good idea, it's not great for your back. Plus, it can become a very messy job, so it's best done in a contained area.

How to change a nappy

- Lie your baby on their back on the changing mat, horizontally to you, with their head by your left hand and their legs by your right (or vice versa if you're left-handed).

- Put a small hand towel underneath your baby, just in case of any unexpected leakages, to avoid having to clean the changing mat cover afterwards.

- Undo their vest and babygrow and fold it under them so that their nappy and bottom half are exposed and well away from any clothing that you want to stay clean and dry.

- Undo the Velcro tabs on the nappy and fold them back onto themselves to avoid scratching your baby.

- Hold your baby's feet up in one hand, gently lifting up their bottom while folding the nappy into itself to keep its contents in place.

- If you have a boy, place a wipe or flannel over their front to avoid any unwanted "water fountain moments". For girls, mid-change wees usually puddle underneath, reinforcing the importance of having a towel to lie on.

- Wet a good-sized clump of cotton wool or a reusable wipe in your bowl of water and use this to clean your baby's bottom, the lower parts of their tummy and back, taking special care of the folds around their groin and thighs. You may need to repeat this process multiple times depending on if it's a number one or two. Remember to always wipe front to back.

- Once baby is wiped clean, remove the dirty nappy and put it to the side to sort out later.

- Use your towel to pat dry your baby's bottom, then fully unfold a clean, fresh nappy and slide it underneath your baby, with the Velcro tabs poking out either side of their hips.

- If there is any redness around their bottom or skin folds, apply a thin layer of nappy cream (don't over-apply, though, as this can cause issues in itself).

- Fold the main nappy flap up to your baby's tummy button and secure the side flaps so they are comfortably flush to your baby's body (not bunched or twisted and not too tight).

- You'll need to be extra careful with your baby's umbilical cord stump while it's still connected. To avoid painful rubbing of the stump, fold down the front of the nappy before securing the Velcro flaps.

- Check that the leg holes of the nappy are suitably snug to your baby to avoid any leakages around the thigh area. If you are using reusable nappies, repeat this process with the waterproof wrap (outer cover), ensuring it is properly secured to prevent leaks.

- Do one final check for any leaks that may have occurred during the changing process before putting your baby's clothes back on.

Poo watch

It can take a day or two for your baby to have their first poo, but when it comes, you're in for a treat. Over the first few weeks of a baby's life, their poo changes colour as their digestive system kicks in, so don't be alarmed by what you find.

- Your baby's first poos should be a gooey, tar-like substance – almost black/very dark green in colour – called meconium, which hardly smells but takes lots of wiping to remove.

- As they drink more, this meconium will flush out of their system and their poo will become runnier, with a grainy mustard-like texture. This usually starts off green before turning more yellow. Again, this doesn't really have any smell.

- Your baby's poos should then settle into more of an orange/light brown colour, though their consistency will vary depending on how you feed them. Breastfed babies generally have runnier poos, while formula-fed babies have firmer, smellier ones.

- While you can usually tell when a nappy needs changing, as it will feel full, heavy or you'll be able to smell it, sometimes it's difficult to know for sure. Most disposable nappies have a wetness indicator line on their front, which changes colour when the nappy is wet.

- Don't leave it too long between changes, or you'll end up having to change not only the nappy but your baby's whole outfit too (which means more hassle and more laundry).

- Never leave your baby unattended while on the changing mat as they could roll off and hurt themselves.

- Most baby vests are designed with an envelope collar, which means it can be put on and removed either by passing it over the baby's head or pulling it down over their bottom – whichever way creates the least mess.

- For easy changing, prioritize babygrows with zips or poppers, and avoid clothing with lots of buttons (which are a real faff).

Making the case for reusable nappies and wipes

Considering the environmental impact each of us has on the planet and the amount of waste an average family creates, more and more parents today are shunning disposable nappies and wipes in favour of reusable cloth alternatives.

Globally, every minute, more than 300,000 disposable nappies are sent to landfill, incinerated or end up as environmental waste, with a standard nappy taking around 500 years to biodegrade, releasing harmful greenhouse gases in the process.

At the same time, disposable wipes are increasingly considered an environmental threat, regularly hitting the headlines for blocking up sewage systems and waterways around the world. Both disposable nappies and wipes also use significantly more energy, materials and water in their manufacturing process than cloth alternatives, adding to their carbon footprint.

While new, more eco-friendly disposable nappies and biodegradable wipes are now available to buy, these are still nowhere near as environmentally friendly as reusables, and they fail to tackle the issue of rising domestic waste.

In contrast, cotton and bamboo cloth nappies and wipes can be used over and over again for many years. Yes, they do require energy and water to wash, but this is in no way comparable to the resources used to make and transport disposables around the world.

With their rising popularity, cloth nappies are also getting cheaper to buy, and there's even a burgeoning second-hand market for these products, which just shows how much they retain their value and usefulness long-term.

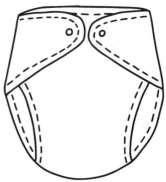

Plus, when they are eventually disposed of, they are completely biodegradable, minimizing their lasting impact on the planet.

Choosing the right reusable nappies

There are lots of different varieties of cloth nappies you can choose from depending on your personal preference, but they usually fall into one of these three categories:

Two-part nappy system – This looks like a disposable nappy but is made of cotton or bamboo, with Velcro straps to secure it in place. It's then covered with a separate waterproof wrap to avoid any leaks. You can buy extra cotton inserts to lay in the nappy to make it more absorbent, for example, during longer stretches at night.

Pros	Cons
• Long lasting, as if one component wears out you only need to replace one element • Best for poo containment (usually only soiling the insert directly under your baby's bum rather than every layer) • Normally has the highest absorbency and least leaks • Can be bought in different sizes to ensure a good fit	• Usually the bulkiest option (requiring a baby vest extender – a small rectangle of cotton with poppers which attaches to your baby's vest, giving more space under their bum) • Can be slower to dry depending on fabric • Slightly slower to put on due to the separate wrap • More expensive as you need to buy the different components separately

Pocket nappy – This nappy is waterproof on the outside with a soft fleece lining on the inside. You can then stuff absorbent inserts into a "pocket" between the waterproof outer layer and fleece lining to increase absorbency.

Pros	Cons
• Quick and easy to change • Usually more slimline than a two-part nappy • One size fits all (thanks to a clever system of poppers), meaning one nappy can last your baby all the way through to potty training	• You need to take time to stuff the clean inserts into the nappy before use, which takes organization ahead of time • Lower containment than a two-part nappy

All-in-one nappy – The nappy and wrap parts are built together into one piece, so there is only one item to wash.

Pros	Cons
• Quickest to change • Easiest for childcare as closest to how a disposable nappy works • Often the most slimline option, not requiring a vest extender	• More prone to leaks as less absorbent than the other options • Can be slow drying, depending on the fabric • If the nappy gets damaged or is overused, the whole thing needs replacing rather than just one part

Whichever variety you choose, check out the sizing options available. Most brands make a newborn size for tiny babies and then a larger size with clever straps and poppers which adjust to fit babies from three to 18 months, meaning you won't need to keep buying larger sizes as your baby grows.

It's recommended that you start off with around 15 to 25 reusable nappies, washing and drying any dirties overnight so they're ready to add back into rotation the next morning. If you find you're running out between washes, buy a few more until you find the right balance for your baby's needs.

DADVICE

When you start using cloth nappies, I recommend buying a few different styles to begin with so you can find the brand and design that works best for you and your lifestyle. Your favourites will quickly emerge, and you can then invest exclusively in those. If the financial investment is a concern, seriously look into second-hand cloth nappies – they are generally well looked after by previous owners or nearly new and are perfectly hygienic once you've washed them. Plus, you can always sell your nappies once you're done with them, making back some of your initial investment.

Reusable wipes

These are simply little squares of cotton towelling which you dampen in water before wiping your baby's bottom. They are quick and easy to use, both at home and when out, and much more effective at doing the job than disposable alternatives. You can buy special packs, which come with a fresh box for the clean ones and a mucky box for the used wipes, or you can simply create your own wipes at home by cutting up an old towel.

Setting up your changing station for reusable nappies and wipes

You can use the same set-up described on page 103, but with a few small changes:

- Swap out the disposable nappies for a supply of reusable cloth nappies, all compiled and ready to use.

- Hang a big waterproof zipped bag on the side of the changing table to store all wet/pee-covered nappies after use to wash later.

- Put a bucket with a lid next to the changing table half filled with water and some washing powder or baby-safe stain remover (for example, Napisan) to soak any nappies that have poo on them. Until your baby starts weaning, their poos will be a runny texture, which will come off easily after a soak. Once they start having more solid poos, it's recommended that you put as much poo as you can down the toilet before putting the nappy into your soak bucket.

- You can put your clean reusable wipes in a sealed box with some water to ensure you have a steady supply of damp wipes ready to go. Alternatively, you can just have a pile of the clean, dry cloths and a bowl of water, wetting each wipe before use.

Washing your reusables

- If you're buying them new, it's recommended that you run all the components through your washing machine three times (without washing powder) before their first use, as this makes them more absorbent.

- When washing reusable nappies and wipes, use washing powder rather than liquid detergent or capsules, and don't use any softener as this can impair the effectiveness of the nappy.

- Wash your dirty nappies and wipes in their own load (not with other items of clothing).

- Don't leave dirty nappies unwashed for more than two days – if you do, it can be hard to get the smell out, even after a wash.

- If your washing machine allows, put the nappies and wipes onto a rinse wash first (just water, to give them a good soak) or use the extra water setting on your machine before washing everything on a 40°C (110°F) cycle.

- Most stains usually come out in the wash, but if any remain, hang the items out in the sun to dry – sunlight naturally bleaches, making any stains magically disappear.

- Ideally, hang your nappies and wipes to dry rather than using a tumble dryer, as this will extend the lifecycle of your reusables.

DADVICE

Don't be afraid to get your hands dirty – baby poo hardly smells and washes off easily in the soak bucket. I recommend rubbing the dirtiest nappies with a reusable wipe or toilet roll to get the worst of the poo off before putting them in your washing machine. You can then dispose of the dirty water down your toilet. If you're worried about poo in your washing machine, don't stress – it all washes away in the process, and you can always check and clean your machine's filter once a month just to be sure.

Bathing your baby

Newborn babies don't need to be bathed every day (two to three times a week is recommended) and it's absolutely fine to wait a few days before giving them their first wash.

Most parents start off with what's known as a "top to tail" wash, where you clean your baby's face, neck, hands and bottom with cotton wool dipped in warm water. While their umbilical stump is still attached and healing, it's advised not to get it wet, so this approach gives you more control over where the water goes.

This type of wash also has the benefit of being quick and easy to do – with your baby lying on a towel and changing mat – avoiding the need for them to be naked for longer than necessary. Keep in mind that babies can get cold very quickly, which is much riskier for them than being a bit dirty, so make sure the room is warm and you have their nappy and clean clothes ready to put on straight after.

It's also important that you use a fresh piece of cotton wool for each part of their body that you clean. And remember, when cleaning your baby's bum:

- For girls, always wipe from front to back, to avoid spreading any germs from the bottom to the vagina.

- For boys, wipe gently around their testicles and penis, but don't pull back the foreskin to clean under there – it's not necessary until they're much older.

Cutting your baby's nails

It always comes as a surprise to new parents just how fast babies' nails grow. If left unchecked, your baby will end up scratching themselves (usually their face) unintentionally. To avoid this, regularly file your baby's nails with a nail file. You can also buy special scissors and nail clippers for babies, though these can be tricky to use (especially if you have a wriggler), leading to you cutting off more nail than intended or, worse still, cutting your baby's fingers.

Looking after your baby's umbilical stump

After your baby's umbilical cord is cut, it remains attached to their tummy button for a week or two. Over this time, it can bleed a little and start to smell, but it will eventually dry out, turn black and fall off, taking another week or so to fully heal. While you wait for this natural process to take place, here are a few pointers to be aware of:

- It's normal for some dried blood to appear on the inside of your baby's nappy where the stump has rubbed. This shouldn't cause your baby any pain.

- Although keeping it dry will help it fall off sooner, don't stress if the stump gets wet while you're washing your baby. Just carefully dry it with a clean towel.

- When the stump falls off, there may be a small amount of sticky discharge where the cord was attached. This can be cleaned with cotton wool and warm water.

Baby's first bath

Once you feel ready to give your baby their first proper bath, there are a few things you'll need to set up.

- Firstly, decide where you are going to bathe them. The best option is to get hold of a special baby bath and stand, which brings the bath up to your waist level, saving your back and making it easy to hold and wash your baby safely. But you can also do it in your own bathtub or even a clean basin if preferred.

- Pick a time that's not straight after a feed when your baby is awake and happy. It's good practice to have bath-time in the early evening, to align with any bedtime routine you might plan to start in the future (see page 176).

- Make sure that both you and your partner are around for these first few bath-times, at least, as it's always helpful to have an extra pair of hands.

- Check the temperature of the water with your elbow **before** putting your baby in. It should feel the same temperature as your skin.

- Hold your baby under their armpits, with their head and shoulders resting on your forearm, and lower them into the water. Alternatively, you can buy moulded bath seats for newborns to lie in, which take some pressure off you needing to physically hold the baby throughout.

- Use your free hand to wash water over their body and a soft sponge or cotton wool for a more thorough clean, remembering to use a new piece of cotton wool for each body part you clean. During their first month, no products are needed – just water.

- Put a warm flannel over your baby's chest and tummy to help keep them warm during their first baths.

- Do get their hair wet and give their scalp a little massage, especially if they have "cradle cap". Just make sure to do this right at the end of their bath to avoid them getting a chill.

- After a few minutes, carefully lift your baby out of the bath and pat them dry with a warm towel, taking extra care to dry under their neck, arms and bottom, around their umbilical stump, and all the folds in their skin, which can get sore if not properly dried.

What is cradle cap?

Cradle cap is a harmless skin condition that forms yellow or white patches on a baby's scalp. Though it doesn't look nice, it isn't painful or itchy for your baby and usually goes away on its own as your baby gets older. However, you can try to make it better by:

- Gently brushing your baby's scalp with a soft hairbrush before you give them a bath, and then washing away any excess flakes that come loose.

- Massaging an emollient cream or coconut oil onto your baby's scalp before bed so it can work its magic while they're asleep.

Keep this up daily and the cradle cap should clear up in a couple of weeks.

Crying – a troubleshooting guide

As amazing as this time will be, it won't be easy. There will be tears, and not just from your baby, as you all adjust to the stresses and strains that come with first-time parenthood. The key to minimizing these down periods is understanding what's causing them, what you can do to turn things around and where to go for help.

Why is my baby crying?

During the first year of your baby's life, but especially in the first six months, crying is their only real form of communication. It doesn't necessarily mean that they're sad, upset or in pain. In most cases, it's just their way of letting you know that they need you, or that something isn't quite right.

Over time, you'll start to recognize the meaning of the different sounds they make, the different cries when they're hungry or tired, or the grunts when they're annoyed or want your attention. But at the beginning, you'll need to become something of a detective to uncover the cause of their screeching.

Helpfully, a baby's cries usually fall into one of the following six categories:

Quick checks and fixes

1. Are they wet?

Does their nappy need changing? Check if a pee, poo or nappy leak could be making them uncomfortable.

2. Are they hungry?

When did they last feed? If it's been 1–2 hours since their last feed, see if they'll breastfeed/take a bottle.

3. Are they tired?

Are they due a nap? If they've been awake for a while, see if they'll go to sleep on you, in the pram or their cot.

4. Are they scared/over-stimulated?

What are you doing together? If there are lots of loud noises, new people or visual stimulation, take them somewhere calmer.

5. Are they wanting attention?

Have they been left alone for long? Try picking them up, reading to them or playing together on a playmat.

6. Are they in pain?

Any signs they are unwell? Check their temperature, try burping them, rubbing their tummy, or giving them a hug.

The first five of these categories are relatively simple to diagnose and correct with quick remedial actions. Number six is always the hardest to figure out. There are so many different reasons why your baby may be uncomfortable or in pain, so let's run through some of the key ones and the actions you can take:

- **Need a burp?** They may have gulped too much air during their last feed which you didn't burp out of them at the time. Put them in the shoulder hold and try some firm taps and circular rubs to their back to see if anything comes out.

- **Feeling gassy or constipated?** Lie your baby on their back and check if their tummy is bloated. If you suspect this may be the case, try giving their tummy a gentle rub in circular motions or hold their legs and help them do little squats and bicycle pedal motions, which can often release trapped gas or encourage a stubborn poo to come out.

- **Feeling congested?** Check if they have a blocked or snotty nose and listen closely to their breathing for any rattling sound. Use saline drops to unblock their nose and put a diffuser or humidifier with vapour oil in their room to help them breathe more easily. If they are struggling to breathe, take them straight to the emergency room.

- **Visible soreness?** Look on their body for any scratches they might have given themselves (due to long nails), dry and cracked skin (usually on their cheeks) or soreness around their bottom or fat folds (i.e. nappy rash) and apply a soothing cream to the affected areas.

For babies over two months old only:

- **Coming down with a fever?** Check their temperature with a digital thermometer and, if it is raised, give them some infant paracetamol to alleviate fever and ease their pain before making an appointment with your doctor.

- **Are they teething?** This process usually doesn't start until your baby is around six months old, but it can occur earlier. Wash your hands and put a finger in their mouth to feel their gums for any signs of baby teeth cutting through. If you think teething is causing your baby pain, give them some liquid paracetamol and invest in some teething gel to rub on their gums.

DADVICE

If none of these investigations shed any light on the problem, and your baby's crying continues, they could be suffering from colic or reflux (see page 144) or something more serious that needs medical assistance. If you are at all worried, always call your doctor and get them checked out by a professional.

Why is my partner crying? The baby blues and beyond

The new baby phase is an emotional rollercoaster for every new mum, in many ways even more intense and gruelling than what she went through during pregnancy. Of course, there are massive highs, but these are balanced out with inevitable lows as she gets to grips with her new role.

Tears are common, especially during the early days after the birth and as the weeks of interrupted sleep finally catch up with her. Tears of joy, sadness, confusion, loneliness, anxiety and exhaustion are all justified in the circumstances, fuelled by hormonal imbalances and other factors outside of her control. If you're able to negotiate paternity leave from your job, take as many days or weeks as you're allowed. Your support will be essential in helping her navigate this challenging time.

While every mother's experience is different, one thing that almost all new mums experience in the days after birth is the "baby blues". Thought to be caused by the sudden chemical and hormonal changes that take place in a mother's body after childbirth, and often being triggered around the time her milk starts to come in, the baby blues can cause your partner to feel low and mildly depressed at a time when she might expect to feel the complete opposite.

The common signs that your partner is experiencing the baby blues include:

- Feeling particularly emotional, irritable or sensitive.
- Crying for no apparent reason.
- Feeling especially anxious, restless and doubting herself.

By knowing what to look out for, you can be on hand to offer extra emotional and physical support during this time, while reassuring her that what she's feeling is entirely normal. The baby blues usually pass by themselves after a few days, after which her general mood should improve.

The baby blues should not be confused with postnatal depression, which is a far more severe condition, affecting around one in ten new mothers. While baby blues consistently strikes at the same time for most mothers, postnatal depression can appear at any point in the first year of your baby's life, developing gradually or suddenly without warning.

What are the signs of postnatal depression?

The symptoms of postnatal depression are not dissimilar to those of the baby blues, but they are generally more severe, last much longer and usually require specialist help to fix. In the worst cases, postnatal depression can stop a new parent from leading a normal life, making them feel incapable of looking after themselves or the baby.

It's important to note that postnatal depression doesn't look the same for everyone, and it can affect dads too. It doesn't make you a bad parent or a bad person. And it doesn't mean you don't love your baby. It's purely a chemical imbalance, not a choice, and often it's difficult to self-diagnose.

Common symptoms to look out for include:

- Not being able to stop crying, and prolonged periods of feeling unable to cope.

- Losing interest in things you would usually enjoy and avoiding any social interaction.

- Being unable to concentrate and regularly experiencing memory loss.

- Extreme tiredness, but being unable to sleep when you have the opportunity.

- Excessive anxiety about your baby and a general feeling of hopelessness.

- Loss of appetite and interest in self-care.

If you're concerned that you or your partner are displaying signs of depression, raise this with your doctor, midwife or health visitor. Don't suffer in silence. There is always help at hand and, with the right support, most people make a full recovery.

How you can help

Whatever your partner is experiencing, there are always things that you can proactively do to help ease her worries and show you care. Let's look at some of the most common triggers that affect a new mother's mood during the first year of parenthood and what us dads can do to help:

Sleep deprivation

A baby's non-stop feeding, changing and sleeping schedule is gruelling, especially for breastfeeding mums. Encourage your partner to go to bed as soon as your baby is down in the evening and take it in turns to change and settle the baby after night feeds. If you can also give your baby a bottle during one of the night feeds, there's no better way to help your partner get a proper stint of quality sleep.

Postpartum pains

Though the birth is over, a new mother's afterpains can be severe, even debilitating, as her uterus contracts. Whether she's had a vaginal delivery, experienced a tear or had surgery, in all instances, she will be in pain as her body recovers. Even breastfeeding can be a painful experience, with shooting pains if your baby latches badly, leading to cracked, sore and bleeding nipples. Keeping on top of pain medication can be difficult in the early newborn fuzz, so take that burden off her and hand-deliver any medication she may be taking, day and night.

Feeling like a milk machine

As amazing as breastfeeding can be for mother-baby bonding, new mums can often feel like they've become a milking machine that's never off duty. If she's also pumping breast milk after each feed to store for later, this just adds to the amount of time she has to dedicate to milk production every day. Maximize your partner's rest and recovery time by bringing the baby to her for every feed, sterilizing the pumping equipment, and decanting and storing the precious breast milk as often as you can.

Overwhelmed

As if the pressure of keeping another human alive wasn't enough, your partner will also be thinking about the million other things on her to-do list, while navigating a near-constant stream of calls, texts, gifts and requests to see the baby from family and friends, which she may feel pressure to respond to. While you're still settling into baby life, continue shouldering the to-do list and try to take on more of the new baby admin yourself.

Feeling self-conscious

Pregnancy and birth are gruelling on a woman's body, with the after-effects ever-present and visible (to her at least) for months to come. Your partner will likely retain some baby weight, have visible scars, excess skin, muscle wastage, pelvic floor weakness and experience hair loss, which might affect her self-esteem. The more reassurance, understanding and affection you can show your partner, and the more time and space you make for her own self-care, the quicker her postpartum recovery should be and the faster her self-confidence should return.

Loneliness

After the initial excitement about your new arrival, the steady stream of visitors and daily check-in calls will slowly die down, to be replaced by the reality check of looking after a baby 24 hours a day, seven days a week. If you return to work while your partner stays home with the baby, this especially can trigger feelings of loneliness. If you can't physically be there, make sure you maintain regular check-in calls and texts throughout the day and offer to take over the baby duties when you get home. Arrange for some home help, if you can, either paid or from a family member, to ensure your partner has extra support (if she wants it).

Feeling underappreciated

Your partner will be putting in crazily long hours of non-stop work, every day, and if you don't make the effort to say thank you and show your appreciation for everything she's been through (and continues to go through), nobody will. This doesn't need to be presents. A kind word, a thoughtful note, an offer of a massage, a bunch of fresh flowers or just a kiss and hug can go a long way.

Why am I crying?!

As modern dads, we're more involved in raising our children and supporting our partners through pregnancy, birth and parenthood than any generation that's come before. Our worry lists are longer. Our workloads are bigger. And the expectations our partners have of us and the pressures we put on ourselves are huge.

Just like our partners, we're spinning countless plates, doing everything we can to make sure none of them drop. Trying to juggle careers and relationships while being active, hands-on dads at the same time, takes a serious amount of energy, patience, effort and stamina. And, with so many additional responsibilities resting on our shoulders, it's easy to become overwhelmed.

If you're feeling this way, you aren't alone. The number of men who become depressed during their first year of fatherhood is double that of the general population, while first-time dads are significantly more vulnerable to postnatal depression than more experienced dads with multiple kids. Because modern fatherhood is hard. And, as men, we aren't always the best at asking for help or admitting when we're struggling.

But, in the same way you've been looking after your partner, you've got to make time to look after yourself. Because if you work yourself to the bone, sacrifice your sleep, get sick, depressed or burn out, your body will force you to make an emergency stop, and you won't be any use to anyone.

This point is so fundamental that I've dedicated an entire chapter to it. Jump forward to Chapter 10 for the full lowdown on how to look after your mind, body and relationship in your new fatherhood role, alongside advice on where to go for help should you ever need it.

Bonding with your baby

Though you might expect to feel an instant connection with your baby, this isn't always the case. It can take some time for fathers and their babies to develop a close bond... and that's okay. You may still be processing the craziness of the birth and what you witnessed your partner go through. Or perhaps you just need some time to get your head around your new role and responsibilities. Whatever your situation, there are lots of things you can do to start building a closer bond with your little one.

Physical contact is key

- Skin-to-skin contact is good for you and calming for your baby, as they feel your warmth and are soothed by your heartbeat. Carrying them around in a sling or baby carrier has a similar effect and is also great for bonding.

- There's nothing quite like the smell of your newborn baby's head, so hold them close and take a good sniff.

- As they're falling asleep, gently stroke their head, cheek or hand to help them feel safe and relaxed. Once they're down, listen out for the little squeaks they make as they dream – there's no better sound in the world.

Make the most of wake windows

- Between naps, your baby might have up to an hour of awake time, so use these wake windows to really engage with them.

- Offer your finger for them to grab in their little hand. It's a special moment you won't forget.

- Though nappy changes and bottle feeding might seem like chores, they're great for bonding as you take responsibility for their care.

- Don't feel embarrassed to have a little chat, sing them a song or make silly faces to see if you can get a reaction. It won't be long before they start smiling and laughing at you, which is guaranteed to melt your heart (if it hasn't already).

How to smash parental leave

If you're lucky enough to get parental leave through your job (mindful that in lots of countries it isn't even offered), grab this opportunity with both hands. It's your chance to be there for your family at the very beginning of this exciting new chapter in your lives.

Though colleagues (usually the older ones) may joke that it's a holiday, asking when you go back to work if you enjoyed your "break", let me tell you... paternity leave is anything but a vacation. You'll work harder than you ever have before, learning new skills every day, while operating on little to no sleep. But, as exhausting as it will be, you won't regret it for a second.

Your time to shine

While during the pregnancy and birth you've largely been an outside observer, this is finally your moment to get your hands dirty and take on a truly hands-on role. Your primary job during parental leave is to look after your partner and new baby, putting into practice all the new skills and practical support you've learned about so far.

But there's a lot more on your to-do list than just looking after them. During parental leave, you'll also need to be a chef, a personal shopper, a cleaner, a nurse, an admin assistant and a gatekeeper, to name but a few of the roles you'll play. So, take a deep breath, roll up your sleeves and plough through every task with positivity, determination and pride. Everything you're doing is for your new family and there's nothing more motivating than that.

To help you along the way, consider these top tips (all personally tried and tested, to great effect), which are guaranteed to take some of the stress out of this busy time:

- Try to leave the house for at least half an hour a day, whether by yourself, as a family unit or just with your baby (to give your partner a proper break). A bit of exercise and fresh air will do you all the world of good.

- Don't be too proud to accept offers of help. Everyone likes to be useful, and pretty much every message you'll receive after your baby's born will say, "If there's anything I can do, just let me know." As your baby gets bigger, those offers will dry up fast, so make the most of them while they're in plentiful supply. Ask friends and family to cook some meals for the freezer, go to the supermarket for you or take the dog for a walk. Anything that can give you time back to rest or just be with your baby.

- Always make a shopping list before going to the supermarket and snap a photo of the inside of your fridge, so you have an instant visual reminder of what you need to buy. This will save you time and money on unnecessary purchases when your tired brain isn't fully engaged on the task.

- Visitors can be exhausting, so discuss with your partner who you want to prioritize for those early visits. Be strict with who you say yes to, when they can come and for how long. And never be afraid to say "no", "not yet", or to ask people to leave so you can get some rest.

- For anyone that does come over, set ground rules and get them to at least wash their hands when they arrive.

- If you don't know them already, learn what the different washing symbols mean on clothing labels so you can confidently do all the laundry yourself (refer to the helpful chart on the next page).

LAUNDRY SYMBOLS

MACHINE WASH NORMAL

MACHINE WASH COLD

MACHINE WASH WARM

MACHINE WASH HOT 50C/120F

MACHINE WASH HOT 60C/140F

MACHINE WASH HOT 70C/160F

MACHINE WASH HOT 90C/200F

MACHINE WASH PERMANENT PRESS

MACHINE WASH GENTLE

HAND WASH NORMAL

BLEACH WHEN NEEDED

NON-CHLORINE BLEACH WHEN NEEDED

DO NOT BLEACH

DRY CLEAN

DO NOT DRY CLEAN

DO NOT DRY

HANG DRY

DRY IN SHADE

DRY FLAT

DRIP DRY

TUMBLE DRY NORMAL

TUMBLE DRY NORMAL LOW HEAT

TUMBLE DRY NORMAL MEDIUM HEAT

TUMBLE DRY NORMAL HIGH HEAT

TUMBLE DRY NORMAL NO HEAT

TUMBLE DRY PERMANENT PRESS

TUMBLE DRY GENTLE NO HEAT

DO NOT TUMBLE DRY

DO NOT DRY

DO NOT WRING

DO NOT IRON

IRON ANY TEMPERATURE STEAM OR DRY

IRON LOW HEAT

IRON MEDIUM HEAT

IRON HIGH HEAT

DO NOT STEAM

Going back to work (or not)

When the time comes for you to return to work after parental leave (if you decide to at all), be mindful that this will be a particularly emotional time for your partner, and quite possibly for you too.

Over the past few days and weeks, the two of you have been a close-knit team, supporting each other and sharing the new baby workload together. But with you out of the picture – for a large chunk of the day at least – it's natural for your partner to feel anxious and worry about how she'll be able to cope with everything on her own.

To make this transition as seamless and worry-free as possible, try the following:

Prepare the ground – Before your first day back, make sure the fridge is fully loaded, the washing pile is tackled and the house is clean, to minimize the extra jobs your partner will need to do on her own during this first transition week without you.

Organize some extra support – If your partner is worried about being left on her own with the baby, try to organize for a grandparent, close friend or maternity nurse (sometimes known as a "mother's help") to come and stay for a few days or even just drop in to provide some extra support while you aren't physically there.

Positive starts – Before you leave for work every day, try to do something thoughtful on your way out of the door.

Happy homecomings – If you're going to be home later than planned, give your partner plenty of advance warning to avoid unnecessary shocks. Bring home something nice for dinner to save on cooking and take over whatever baby duties you can as soon as you walk through the door.

If you're being paid to work full time outside of the home and your partner is working full time at home raising your baby, consider the following:

- Think of yourselves as having two distinct jobs – your paid job (doing whatever you do to bring in the family's income) and your partner's unpaid one (focused on childcare and household tasks). Both jobs are equally valuable and a Monday to Friday deal, with the same hours worked. When you're both at home in the morning, evening and weekends, the job of childcare and household tasks is a team effort, split between you. Just because one parent works outside of the home and receives a salary, it doesn't mean the parent at home should work 24/7.

- Be responsive to calls and messages from home during the working day, so your partner doesn't feel forgotten or unsupported. And check in regularly if you haven't heard anything.

- If your partner gets ill, try to find someone to help with the baby at home, or better yet, ask to take some sick or compassionate leave yourself until they get better. If you wouldn't go to work when ill, they shouldn't be expected to.

- You'll want to have fun with your baby when you get home from work, but avoid getting them over-excited – they need a calm environment before they go to sleep.

- Don't expect a thank you for being hands-on – your partner will have gone the whole day at home without any recognition for their hard work, so praising you might not be front of mind. Show gratitude daily and you're more likely to get it back.

Ultimately, don't live to regret prioritizing work over your family during these formative early years. Because while you may love your job, there's no career on the planet more rewarding, more life-affirming and more important than being a dad.

Another way – tales of a stay-at-home dad
(Gavin's story)

During my wife's pregnancy with our first child, we broached the subject of me taking on the fun and games of being a stay-at-home dad. We weighed up what we both earned, and it quickly became apparent that if I stayed in work, the majority of my salary would go straight into the pockets of someone else to take care of our daughter. This made no sense to me, so I resolved to take on the mantle of full-time carer. What could possibly go wrong?

Everything I've done in my life has had an element of risk to it. I rarely follow the well-trodden path. In fact, you might say my life has always been something of a paradox. I'm an ex-ballet dancer who plays and teaches blues rock guitar. A guy who loves cleaning almost as much as I like riding fast motorbikes. A *will-he-ever-bloody-stop-and-just-sit-down-for-a-minute* type person with boundless energy, as well as being a congenital heart disorder sufferer who's had two open-heart surgeries. And an improviser who tries to stay open and adapt to whatever's happening, while also being a massive control freak.

I believe it's this adaptability that makes full-time parenting work for me.

Being a stay-at-home dad means being everything all at once, all of the time. There's a flexibility and a freedom to it, unlike any job you've had before. I can set my own rules, shifting and redefining them at my leisure to suit my natural, paradoxical interests and personal views on life.

The toughest part for me has been suppressing my natural, rather male inclination to want to control and fix everything. As a full-time parent, this is an almost impossible task. One minute you think you've got into some kind of routine or habit, and the next everything invariably gets turned upside down by some unexpected turn of events. Adaptability is vital.

You also need to be fully committed to the role. I had this epiphany while looking at a photo of our unborn daughter after our first sonogram. It dawned on me that, for the first time, my life would be completely and utterly about someone else. I wouldn't be able to fix or control everything as I so dearly wanted to. My job was to be there for her, to guide her when she starts eating, walking, falling, sharing toys, having arguments with her friends or the myriad of life challenges she'll face in the years to come. I knew in that moment, beyond any doubt, that I wanted to be around for every single moment.

Other dads often come up to me saying they're quite envious of my set-up. I get it. The good times (and there are many) are exquisite. Funny. Inspiring. Just plain silly. But the hard times (and there are many of those too) are really hard. Harder than anything I've done before (and I've had to wear a jockstrap, tights and make-up for a living).

But I wouldn't have it any other way. Now a stay-at-home dad of two, I see how special my relationships are with my children. I've witnessed every "first", been with them for every high and low, and learned so much about myself in the process.

We've become a little army, thick as thieves, with a bond I wouldn't exchange for the world. And I'm so glad I've had this opportunity. Because there will come a time, in the not-too-distant future, when they won't need me so much, and I won't see them every day.

But all that is for another day. Right now I choose to live like they do... totally in the present and making the most of every minute we have together.

Gavin is a teacher, guitarist and writer, who has been a stay-at-home dad for the past seven and a half years. He lives in London with wife Victoria, kids Layla and Axel, dogs Ralf and Albert, and cat Atticus.

Call to arms (sharing the parenting load)

Parenting really is one of the toughest, least appreciated and most physically and mentally exhausting jobs around. And yet, society still massively undervalues the huge amount of work it takes to raise the next generation.

You might have heard the phrase, "It takes a village to raise a child." And back in the day, that's exactly how it was. New parents had so much more child-rearing support from family, friends, neighbours and the wider community than we do today. It was also much more possible to live off one salary and still afford regular childcare, buy a house, pay the bills and go on holiday.

But the reality is that modern incomes don't cover what they used to, while societal expectations on new parents (especially new mothers) are greater than they've ever been. Not only is the parenting role itself bigger, but more of the invisible, unpaid tasks associated with raising a family and modern life fall on new parents to complete themselves, with the so-called "village" nowhere to be seen.

Given that gender inequality at work is still commonplace, with men earning more (on average) than women with the same skills and experience, the bulk of the parenting and domestic load is often heavily biased against women.

As modern fathers, we shouldn't just accept this as the status quo. It's unreasonable to expect the weight of childcare responsibilities to land solely on a mother's shoulders. Add to this all the other daily tasks we all need to complete just to get through the day – the laundry, shopping, cleaning, cooking and general life admin – and it's even more unrealistic to expect one person to do it all alone.

You might think the solution here is to work harder, to earn more money and be able to afford the parenting lifestyle of previous generations. But don't underestimate the years this will take to accomplish, the strains you'll put your family under and the moments you'll miss in pursuit of financial security. Your partner and your child need you now, and the more hands-on you can be during these earlier years the bigger the benefits will be for everyone.

Juggling fatherhood and a career

If employers aren't recognizing the realities of modern parenthood, it's up to us to change the narrative in the workplace.

How we each do this will depend on our own personal ambitions, priorities, type of job and financial security. You might feel able to go big and make a stand, or you might prefer or need to go for the little wins. Whatever you decide, just remember that any positive changes you can push through will benefit everyone now and in the future.

- Correct colleagues who joke about parental leave being "time off" – raising a baby is anything but a break and referring to it as such does no favours for parents pushing for more parental benefits.

- If your financial situation allows, ask if you can take extra time away from work when your baby is small, even if it's unpaid. It will be a financial hit, but equally, this is a special time in your life that you'll never get back.

- Find out if you can work flexible hours – coming in later or leaving early – so you can be at home for the busiest times of the day. It will be a huge support for your partner and give you more time to bond with your baby while setting a positive precedent in years to come when you need to drop off/pick up your child from nursery or school.

- Help your employer understand the business benefits that flexible working for parents can bring them, in terms of increased efficiency, focus, productivity, morale and loyalty from their parenting workforce.

- When leaving work to be with your family, don't apologize or sneak away – "leave loudly", so colleagues know that parenting responsibilities are nothing to be ashamed of.

- Be strict with yourself about not constantly checking your phone when you get home from work. Separating work and family time is the only way to stay sane. See page 272 for more advice on finding your work/life balance.

Benefits of being a hands-on dad

Build a stronger relationship with your partner

The more hands-on you are, both with your baby and with domestic family life, the more you will:

- help your partner feel more supported and understood, aid her postpartum recovery, give her much-needed breaks throughout the day and night, and create a happier home environment as a result.

- experience first-hand the joys and frustrations of baby life and see for yourself how much work goes into caring for a baby.

- appreciate your partner, truly recognize the sacrifices she's made and never assume that your day at work was more tiring than hers.

- be better equipped to recognize when your partner is struggling or overwhelmed and provide the extra support she needs in the moment.

- show your other half that you are in this together, building a closer connection and team dynamic, giving her more confidence and space to figure out what kind of mother she wants to be.

Develop a closer and lasting bond with your baby

By being actively involved in your baby's care, you will:

- become a key person in their life that they recognize, respond to and love unconditionally.

- learn to recognize their cries and the different sounds they make, and be able to give them what they want and need at any given moment.

- avoid missing out on the key moments in their development, like their first smile, first words and first steps.

- help your baby feel more safe and secure while teaching them new skills and values to live by, shaping the person they will become.

Increase your own parenting confidence and give new purpose to your life

Being a hands-on dad will teach you so much about yourself and the type of person you aspire to be while giving you the kind of confidence, purpose and drive that only comes when everything you do is out of love for someone else. It will help you:

- learn new skills, both baby-related and more general life skills, from changing a nappy to better organizing your time.
- feel confident and in control when alone with your baby, unfazed by whatever challenges you might face.
- have pride in your work at home, knowing you're doing something hugely positive for your family.
- always have a reason to get up in the morning, work hard and do your best.

Take on gender inequality and pave the way for future fathers

Being a hands-on dad isn't only good for us, our partners and our babies; it's got wide-reaching benefits to society as a whole too. The more we show the world we're capable and the more parental responsibilities we take on:

- the more society will recognize the important role we play in our children's lives, changing outdated stereotypes of fatherhood for good.
- the more employers will recognize this too, helping make the case for improved benefits for parents in the workplace.
- the better example we'll be setting for new dads that come after us.
- the less our partners will have to sacrifice their own job or career, knowing that the childcare responsibilities are equally shared.
- the less women will be held back at work in terms of promotions and pay rises just for being a mother.

"WHAT WE BECOME DEPENDS ON WHAT OUR FATHERS TEACH US AT ODD MOMENTS, WHEN THEY AREN'T TRYING TO TEACH US."

Umberto Eco

CHAPTER 5

FEEDING YOUR BABY

You may well wonder – as someone who's genetically incapable of breastfeeding yourself – where you fit into this equation. But let me tell you, the role you will play in feeding your baby over the coming months and years will be so important, setting your little one up to have a healthy relationship with food for years to come.

If your partner decides to give breastfeeding a go, your support will be invaluable. Breastfeeding may sound simple enough, but as every new parent soon realizes, it's a lot harder than it looks. It takes patience, commitment, stamina and teamwork to get it right, and every mother's experience is different. But the more informed you are and the more support you can provide, the greater chance you'll both have of making a success of it.

While lots of healthcare professionals and other parents may put pressure on your partner to breastfeed, it's important to know that breastfeeding isn't the only way to feed a baby. There are countless healthy, happy and successful adults who turned out just fine without ever having been breastfed.

There's no one-size-fits-all approach here, so in this chapter we'll cover every option available to you while giving you all the information and tools you'll need to make a success of this long and often complicated feeding journey. Not just in the first six months of your baby's life, when milk is the only thing on the menu. We'll also delve into the world of weaning, looking at how and when to start introducing your baby to new tastes and textures, the kit you'll need, alongside lots of practical advice on everything from food allergies to fussy eaters.

The most important thing to remember is that feeding a child isn't solely a mother's job. There's so much to think about and organize, from round-the-clock feeding schedules, bottle sterilizing and bib management, to food shopping, menu planning and cooking; far too much for one person to shoulder on their own. It should be a team effort, so do your research and get involved... it's going to be one messy ride.

How to be the world's best breastfeeding wingman

Breastfeeding is more likely to succeed if both you and your partner know the ropes and can work together as a team. As a dad, you obviously don't have the nature-given assets to breastfeed, but there's a huge amount of organization and admin around breastfeeding that you can get involved in to support your partner.

Inform yourself – Two minds are always better than one, so do your research, learn about different breastfeeding holds, what a good latch looks like and what solutions to try if something isn't working.

Special delivery – Bring the baby to mum when it's time to feed, to save your partner from having to use up energy unnecessarily, especially if she had a C-section or postnatal surgery.

Set them up – Help your partner get in a comfortable position for every feed. Find her nursing pillow, puff up the cushions around her, get her a blanket if it's cold and bring her a drink and snack to stay hydrated and keep her energy levels up.

TOP TIP

Setting up a breastfeeding snack basket

A breastfeeding mum should be consuming around 400 calories more than usual every day to help maintain her milk supply. But, as any new parent will tell you, it can be surprisingly easy to forget to eat or drink for hours on end when you have a hungry baby to contend with.

Put together a basket of edible treats for your partner and keep it near where she usually breastfeeds, topping it up daily. Raid the kitchen cupboards and local store for a wide selection of snacks, ready for mum to pick at during a feed or whenever her energy levels are running low.

Keep her company – Breastfeeding can be quite a lonely activity, so don't just leave her to it (unless she specifically wants you to). Talk to her. Offer her a foot rub. Or even just make sure the TV remote is within reaching distance.

Teamwork is key – During every feed, your partner will effectively be stuck in one place for up to an hour at a time, incapable of doing much else. If your partner doesn't need you in the room with her, try to be as useful as possible by completing a job around the house that needs doing to lighten her to-do list.

Finish the job – The feeding process involves more than just the breastfeeding itself, so help out where you can. Change your baby's nappy, burp them and settle them to sleep, so these extra tasks don't always fall on the mum.

Master scheduler – Keeping track of timings of feeds and breast logistics is a full-time job. During the first two weeks at least, help your partner out by writing down the timings of each feed and nappy change (Wet? Poo? What colour?), how long your baby fed on each breast and which breast your baby fed on first.

Be on the lookout – If something's wrong, the person closest to the problem can often be the last to notice. Your partner will be so focused on the baby that she may neglect to look after herself. Keep a supportive eye on your partner's physical and mental health and encourage her to ask for help if she's struggling.

Doing things like this will help your partner feel comfortable, relaxed and cared for, which in turn will support breast milk production while giving her the time and space she needs to recover from the birth and focus on the job at hand.

Breastfeeding – everything you need to know

Starting out

The first few weeks of breastfeeding are often the most stressful. Both mum and baby are learning a new skill, which doesn't always click right away. As your partner's milk "comes in", your baby will have to get to grips with the switch from small volumes of colostrum to large servings of breast milk. At the same time, the whole process can be emotionally draining and physically painful for your partner, as her nipples get accustomed to a baby feeding from them eight to 15 times per day.

Although this intense feeding schedule is entirely normal, lots of new parents worry that their baby is feeding so often because they aren't getting enough to drink. Don't worry. Over the coming weeks, the more your baby feeds, the more breast milk your partner should produce, as her breasts naturally tailor milk supply to demand. As this happens, you should notice more and more wet nappies and regular runny poos, which indicate that your baby is getting plenty of milk.

A well-fed baby should also:

- look calm and sleepy after feeds;
- gradually gain weight (20–30 g/0.7–1 oz per day after an initial period of weight loss); and
- only want a feed every one to three hours (although cluster feeding – when your baby wants lots of short feeds over a few hours – is also entirely normal, usually during growth spurts in the first four months).

DID YOU KNOW?

Breast milk is magical stuff, containing natural antibiotic healing properties that can be applied to baby's and mum's skin to treat dryness, cuts and scrapes. It also has an amazing ability to adapt to your baby's needs, becoming more watery if your baby is dehydrated or adding specific antibodies to fight infections.

The importance of a good latch

How your baby latches onto your partner's breast is crucial for efficient feeding and to avoid unnecessary pain and suffering for your partner.

While your partner and baby are still learning how to breastfeed, your support in getting your baby into the right position and spotting a good or bad latch can be hugely valuable, so make sure you know what to look out for and what alternatives to suggest if something isn't working.

Best positions for breastfeeding

Cradle hold

Rugby-ball hold

Laid-back hold

Cross-cradle hold

Side-lying hold

Achieving the perfect latch

- Your baby should be in one of the holds on the previous page, with their body in close contact to your partner's.

- She should support the back of baby's neck – not the back of their head, as you want your baby to maintain some flexibility in their neck.

- Your partner should let your baby's head tip back slightly, gently stroking baby's nose and top lip with the nipple so they can smell the breast milk.

- She should then wait for your baby's mouth to open wide and guide their chin to touch the breast first before rolling their face forward to latch onto it.

- If your partner is finding the latch painful or your baby only has the tip of the nipple, she should gently put a clean finger in your baby's mouth to break the suction, un-latch and try again.

- Most importantly, it's always better to get the latch right from the outset than for your partner to feed through the pain.

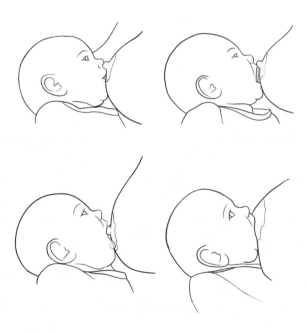

Signs of a good latch

- The latch feels comfortable and pain free (give it 10–20 seconds to see if it settles).

- Your baby's cheeks look full and puffed out as they feed.

- All of your partner's nipple is in the baby's mouth – you might see just a bit of the areola above your baby's top lip but less or none below.

- Your baby's head, neck and back should be in alignment, not twisted to one side.

- You hear or see your baby swallowing (if you hear a ticking or clicking sound while your baby is drinking, suggest that your partner tries to re-latch, as this is a sign that baby is taking in excess air).

Once your baby has successfully latched, they should feed solidly until they have had enough. Your partner should then give the baby a burp, before turning them around and offering them a feed from her other breast. On average, a newborn baby might feed for between 10 and 20 minutes on each side, though there is no hard and fast rule, with every baby's needs being unique and different. As they get older and more skilled at breastfeeding, the length of each feed usually reduces.

Often a baby will feed less from the second breast, so it should be offered to your baby first for their next feed to ensure both breasts are getting equal attention throughout the day. Doing this can help to regulate her milk supply in both breasts and avoid nasty side effects like mastitis, a painful infection caused by blocked milk ducts.

Even if mum is doing everything right, your baby may still get frustrated during a feed, crying and fussing or even detaching themselves altogether and refusing to feed. Usually, this is due to one of the following reasons:

- Your baby may have a virus or blocked nose – babies are nose breathers, so try clearing a nostril with saline solution to help their breathing and take frequent rests during each feed.

- Your partner's milk tastes different after eating certain foods – curries and spicy foods are particularly potent, so some mums try to avoid them while breastfeeding.

- Too many visual distractions – try moving to a quieter, dimly lit space to feed, or use a breastfeeding cover or muslin draped over your partner's shoulder and baby's head to make the feeding space less distracting.
- If your baby has started teething and their gums are tender, apply some numbing teething gel to their gums before each feed.
- Your baby may have colic or reflux, which can make feeding more of a struggle.

Then again, sometimes there may be no obvious reason. If so, encourage your partner to take a break and try again a bit later.

DADVICE

While a bit of fussiness is normal, if your baby is regularly refusing the breast and you're concerned, always seek advice from a healthcare professional or breastfeeding specialist.

What are colic and reflux, and are they treatable?

Colic

If your baby cries for long periods of time for no obvious reason and is difficult to console, chances are they may have colic. It usually strikes suddenly during the first four months of a baby's life and has no known cause.

All you can do in this situation is try to soothe your baby as best as you can:

- Cuddle and gently rock them when they're crying (colicky babies often prefer to spend more time upright in a sling or baby carrier).
- Hold them upright during and after feeds, to minimize the amount of extra air they swallow.

- Thoroughly burp them after every feed, ideally upright, over your shoulder.
- Rock them to sleep in your Moses basket, crib or in their pram rather than in a static environment.

Reflux

If your baby is regularly sicking up milk during or soon after feeding, or they are coughing, hiccupping or crying during feeds and not settling afterwards, they may be suffering from reflux. This is a common condition, which affects babies from eight weeks old and usually clears up on its own during their first year.

To help a reflux baby keep down the milk they drink and avoid losing weight, you'll usually be advised to:

- Hold your baby in an upright position for as long as possible after feeding.
- Burp them more thoroughly, both during their feeds and afterwards.
- Try feeding them smaller feeds more often (especially if bottle feeding).

If none of these make a difference, speak to your health visitor or doctor, who will be able to advise if special medication or alternative milk substitutes are needed.

> **DADVICE**
>
> If it's found that your baby does have colic or reflux, be sure to give your partner lots of additional emotional support. Navigating these feeding challenges can be extremely stressful and distressing, especially for new mums.

A painful business

Most new mums experience nipple tenderness and soreness in the first few weeks after birth. This should settle down as your partner's breasts and nipples get conditioned to breastfeeding, but cracked, blistered and even bleeding nipples are still common.

These afflictions can make every feed extremely painful, regardless of how good the latch is, causing some new mums to develop a fear of breastfeeding and ultimately move onto bottle feeding earlier than planned.

TOP TIP

If your partner has sore nipples, she can apply some of her breast milk or a lanolin nipple cream after every feed, which helps soothe and heal them between shifts. Cold compresses are also extremely soothing, so put some cotton breast pads and cabbage leaves (yes, actual leaves from a cabbage) in the freezer and grab her two to put in her nursing bra between feeds.

If you've checked the latch, tried different nursing positions and are treating her sore nipples, but breastfeeding is still proving extremely painful for your partner, there are a few other things you should look into:

Does your baby have thrush?

If pain is affecting both breasts and intensifies throughout the feed, or if your partner has itchy breasts, check inside your baby's mouth for white spots and around their bottom for a persistent nappy rash with sore-looking spots. These symptoms could indicate your baby has oral thrush, a common infection that can be quickly and easily treated (if it doesn't clear up on its own). Just ensure both your partner and baby get treatment at the same time to avoid reinfection.

Does your baby have a tongue tie?

This is where the strip of skin connecting your baby's tongue to the bottom of their mouth is shorter than usual, which can make it harder for them to latch efficiently. Depending on the severity of the tongue tie, your baby may have no problems feeding, but in extreme cases, it might require a (very quick and relatively painless) surgical procedure to correct.

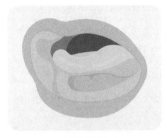

NORMAL

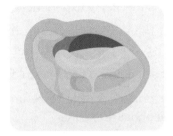

TONGUE TIE

Does your partner have mastitis?

Caused by poor milk drainage, mastitis is an inflammation of breast tissue which can result in pain, swelling, warmth and redness in the breast, with your partner experiencing a high temperature and chills. In the very worst cases, mastitis can develop into sepsis, so always seek medical advice if your partner is experiencing these symptoms.

> ### DADVICE
>
> If your partner suffers from mastitis, she will need lots of extra support from you around feeds until it resolves itself. Encourage her to continue breastfeeding throughout, bringing her paracetamol and lots of fluids to bring down any fever, ibuprofen to manage her pain and hot and cold compresses to improve her milk flow. Run her a hot bath every day (if you have one) so she can carefully massage the affected breast (stroking from the top of the breast towards her nipple) to try and unblock the infected milk ducts.

Bottle feeding

While the breast vs bottle debate is highly contentious, there are many very valid reasons why your partner may choose to bottle feed your baby using pumped breast milk or formula instead of exclusively breastfeeding:

- Your partner's milk supply doesn't match your baby's demand (most commonly if she experienced a particularly traumatic birth).
- Your baby is losing weight and requires extra top-ups of expressed breast milk or formula to get back on track.
- Breastfeeding is too painful for your partner.
- Your partner needs to return to work and your baby is in your (or someone else's) care.
- Your baby has a tongue tie or high palate, making breastfeeding more difficult.
- Breastfeeding is negatively affecting your partner's mental health.
- Your baby has certain allergies or health concerns that need a specific formula-based diet.
- Your baby is teething and prone to biting your partner's breast during feeds.
- You want to do some of the feeds yourself to give your partner a break.
- Your partner may just choose not to breastfeed.

Whatever you decide, nobody should be made to feel guilty about the choices they make here. At the end of the day, a well-fed baby and a happy mum are the most important things, no matter which option you choose.

Different types of bottle feeding

Depending on your personal situation, you can bottle feed your baby from birth using either expressed breast milk from your partner or a donor, or first infant formula.

Either option can be used exclusively, or you can "combination feed" (switching between breast milk and formula, using either a bottle for every feed or a combination of breast and bottle).

If you do switch between breastfeeding and bottle feeding, just be aware that some babies can experience something called "nipple confusion", which can prevent them from breastfeeding going forward.

What is nipple confusion?

Breastfed babies have a specific suck pattern to get milk from the breast, which is different to how they drink from the teat of a baby bottle (which is generally more fast flowing). This different technique can cause some babies to get a little lost when switching between a mother's breast and a bottle's teat, with some preferring the ease of feeding from a bottle. While this can lead to them rejecting the breast altogether, it should be noted that not all bottle-fed babies get nipple confusion, and many can happily transition between breast and bottle with ease.

Breast pumps and expressed milk

If you plan on bottle feeding your baby using expressed milk, you'll need to invest in a breast pump. While your partner can express milk by hand, the time it takes to fill a bottle is usually not worth the effort. Thankfully, breast pumps are readily available online, can be bought or hired second-hand, or even loaned from your hospital. For maximum milk extraction, a double pump (which can express milk from both breasts at the same time) is recommended.

If your partner is breastfeeding while also expressing milk using a breast pump, it's advised that she pump after every breastfeed rather than before. If she only pumps once or twice in a day, depending on how much expressed milk she needs, it's also recommended that she pump in the early hours of the morning when her supply is usually the greatest.

How you can help

- Before every pumping session, take charge of sterilizing the pump and its components so they are ready to go when your partner needs them.

- Take the baby after each breastfeed and settle them, so your partner can pump in peace. Be aware, pumping usually takes around 15 minutes per breast (though how much she produces and how long it takes will depend on your partner's supply).

- When she's finished pumping, help her detach from the pump and be extra careful not to spill anything she's just expressed (it's precious stuff and you won't want to waste a drop).

- Take charge of decanting the milk into a special storage bag or bottle, and store correctly with a label saying how much and when it was pumped.

Safe storage

Freshly expressed breast milk can be stored safely at room temperature for up to four hours, in the fridge for up to four days or in the freezer for six months (ideal if your partner is going back to work and you need a big supply). When you need it, refrigerated or frozen breast milk can then be warmed in a bowl of hot water before being bottle-fed to your baby.

DID YOU KNOW?

Breast milk looks quite different to what you might expect. Unlike white cow's milk, expressed breast milk can look watery, with a slightly blue tone, and when it's stored in a bottle, the fat rises to the top (so it needs to be shaken before serving).

On the subject of cow's milk, babies shouldn't drink this until they are at least 12 months old. It doesn't have the right nutrients that your baby needs, with too many proteins and minerals for smaller baby's kidneys to process.

Formula feeding

Many parents use formula instead of breast milk to feed their baby. This comes either:

- ready mixed, which you decant into a baby bottle; or
- in powder form, which you mix with boiled/sterile water before cooling.

While ready-mixed formula is convenient, especially when you're on the go, it's significantly more expensive than the powdered alternative, so most parents mainly use the latter. You should use first infant formula from newborn to 12 months, though there are different varieties you can buy from six months (for example, with added vitamins), depending on the specific needs of your baby.

Always carefully check the label to make sure it's suitable, and to confirm how much powder to use and what quantities your baby should drink at different stages. This varies depending on what brand you buy.

It's also generally considered to be more filling than breast milk, meaning formula-fed babies often demand a feed less often and sleep longer as they're more "full up". However, on the flip side, your baby's poos will be smellier and have a thicker consistency if they're formula-fed.

TOP TIPS

- Never give your baby a bottle without checking the temperature of the milk first, by putting a few drops on your wrist or the back of your hand. It should feel warm, not hot.

- Always put a bib on your baby to protect their clothes from sicked-up or spilled milk.

- Hold the bottle so the teat is filled with milk, to avoid your baby sucking in air, which will make them gassy.

- If your baby falls asleep on the bottle or stops feeding too early, gently blow on their face to wake them up or try tickling under their chin, which can activate their natural suckling action, getting them to keep drinking.

Sterilizing

It's important that you sterilize your baby's bottles and teats before every feed until they're at least six months old, to protect your baby against infections. There are three main ways you can do this:

1. Invest in a microwave-compatible or electric sterilizer which steam cleans your baby feeding equipment. This is by far the quickest, most convenient option. Just follow the manufacturer's instructions, as each sterilizer is different.

2. Boil your feeding equipment in a large saucepan of water for ten minutes, ensuring it all stays under the surface throughout. Although no special equipment is needed for this method, it's worth being aware that bottles and teats sterilized in this way tend to get damaged faster.

3. Buy cold water sterilizing solution (either ready mixed or in tablet form, which you dissolve in water) and submerge your feeding equipment in this for at least 30 minutes. This option is ideal for holidays or weekends away.

After you've finished sterilizing, you can leave your bottles and teats in the sterilizer or saucepan until you need them. If you do take them out, wash your hands first or use sterile tongs before compiling the bottles, and make sure you put their lids on straight away to avoid contamination.

When to start weaning and how to do it

For the first year of your baby's life, milk will be their main source of hydration and nutrition. However, from six months, you can start introducing your baby to new tastes and textures (known as complementary feeding), before gradually introducing a wider variety of solid foods as you prepare them for a healthy relationship with food for years to come.

Stage 1
Complementary feeding (age 6–8 months)

Complementary feeding is not about reducing your baby's milk intake, but rather letting your baby try certain foods alongside their normal breast or bottle feeds. By doing this, your baby can start to get used to different flavours and textures, before learning how to chew and swallow solid foods and feed themselves (known as baby-led weaning).

Most government guidelines advise starting this process when your baby is around six months old, as by then they should be able to move food around their mouth and safely swallow it, reducing the risks of choking. It's recommended that you start with baby porridge and easy-to-swallow vegetable purees, gradually introducing them into your baby's diet around their usual feeding routine. If you want to try baby-led weaning, you can also offer them soft finger foods at this stage, such as cooked carrot or peeled cucumber sticks.

The goal here is familiarization, not calorie intake. Start off trying one or two meals per day in very small quantities (a couple of teaspoons is plenty). When they start swallowing more than they spit out, you can gradually increase the quantity you feed them while maintaining their usual breast or bottle feeds as normal. From six months, you can also offer your baby sips of water from a cup or beaker with their meals.

Recommended kit you'll need

- Highchair (with in-built tray, ideally)
- Long-sleeved bib (to protect their clothes from spills)
- Waterproof bucket bibs (to catch any food they spit out or drop)
- Soft weaning spoons
- Sippy cup (with a teat at this stage)
- Ice cube trays (to freeze individual portions of homemade puree)
- Baby food steamer/processor (if you have the budget and plan on making your own purees)

DADVICE

Get involved in making purees at home and feeding your baby whenever you can. It's quick and easy to do, plus you'll save money, take pressure off your partner and get more bonding time with your baby, so it's worth your while.

Get started by buying some root vegetables, which are ideal for this first stage of weaning. Steam a carrot, half a swede and a parsnip until soft (steaming is better than boiling as it maintains more of the vegetables' nutrients). Once the vegetables are cooked and suitably soft, puree the whole lot together, allow it to cool, then spoon the orangey mix into an ice cube tray and freeze. Once frozen, the individual cubes can be defrosted in the microwave when needed as a quick and easy meal.

Stage 2
Introducing new tastes and textures (8–10 months)

Now that your baby has a few teeth and is comfortable eating smooth textured foods, you can start to introduce more complex, lumpier purees to get them used to solids, as well as a wider variety of finger foods to encourage independent feeding.

Variety is key here to keep things interesting. Think about different tastes, textures and colours you can give your baby, which should encourage them to be more adventurous with food and open to trying new things in future. Easy options to try include:

- Mashed fruit and cooked/steamed vegetables rather than purees
- Soft, cooked white meats or flaky fish (either on their own as finger foods or blended with vegetables in a puree)
- Vegetable batons and sliced-up fruit
- Peas (cooked or frozen)
- Breadsticks, rice cakes and oatcakes
- Dairy products, like yoghurt and soft pasteurized cheese
- Bread and toast soldiers

At this stage, your baby can now have two to three small meals a day, gradually increasing the quantity they eat depending on their appetite. As they are taking in more calories from food now, you can gradually start to decrease the amount of milk they drink (always being mindful to follow their lead here, rather than forcing it).

DADVICE

It's normal for babies to gag from time to time during this weaning stage as they figure out how to chew their food properly. Never leave your baby unattended when they're eating, just in case they start choking and need your help. For this reason, don't give your baby snacks in the car unless you're physically sitting in the back seat with them.

What to do if your baby chokes

It's highly recommended that all new parents take an annual first aid course to learn the basics of CPR and what to do when your baby is choking. Usually, a few firm slaps between their shoulder blades will dislodge any food that gets stuck, but if not:

- Quickly remove your baby from their highchair and position them face down across your thighs, making sure their head is lower than their chest.

- With your hand under their chest, give five firm back blows between their shoulder blades with the heel of your hand.

- If the item still hasn't dislodged, turn your baby over so they're lying face up on your thighs, cradling their head in your hand, with their head lower than their chest.

- Using the pads of your fingers, give your baby five chest thrusts in the centre of their chest.

- Repeat this process of back blows and chest thrusts until the object is dislodged.

- If in doubt, call the emergency services, and they can talk you through it and send help.

Stage 3
Preparing for family food (10–12 months)

At this stage, your baby is ready to broaden their food horizons as they gear up to make the switch from milk dependency to solid foods after their first birthday. They can now enjoy three solid meals a day, eating more complex and complete recipes similar to what you're having (just smaller portions, cut up and unseasoned – i.e. avoiding salt and sugar).

Of course, you can still give them the baby porridge, purees and yoghurts they've enjoyed over recent months. But, with more teeth to handle crunchier, firmer foods and their stomachs more developed, they can now eat most food types, including heavier proteins like red meat.

During this stage, they will still have regular breast milk or formula feeds – aiming for around 500 ml (17.5 fl oz) total per day – though food is now an important part of their diet and nutrient intake.

While they will be too young to use cutlery, you should encourage them to feed themselves more and more, and you can give them a soft spoon to play with during feeds to get familiar with it.

Stage 4
Year one and beyond

Once your baby is 12 months old, solid food should be their main source of nutrition and calories. If your partner is breastfeeding, she can continue doing this for a while yet if she wants to, or you can replace formula with full-fat cow's milk from this stage onwards (a minimum of 350 ml/12 fl oz milk or two servings of dairy products per day).

Otherwise, a healthy mix of fruit and vegetables, protein (meat, fish, eggs or plant-based) and starchy food (such as potatoes, bread and rice) will ensure your child is getting everything they need.

Foods to be careful with

Avoid	Potential choking hazards
• Popcorn (not recommended under four years old)	• Grapes
• Low-fat, skimmed or raw milk	• Strawberries
• Salty and sugary food	• Cherry tomatoes
• Honey (not recommended if under one)	• Baby carrots
• Raw fish	• Baby corn
• Saturated fat	• Sausages
• Anything with bones	• Marshmallows
	Always cut these foods into manageable chunks

Allergic reactions

When introducing your baby to new foods, it's impossible to know whether they might have any undiagnosed food intolerances or allergies that could trigger an allergic reaction. But, if you have a family history of certain allergies, there is a greater chance your baby will too.

It's recommended that you start to introduce your baby to common allergen foods (such as eggs, peanut butter, soya, cow's milk and fish) once they hit the six-month mark, as evidence suggests there's a higher probability of developing an allergy to these foods if you leave it any longer.

When you do, try each food one at a time, in tiny quantities, keeping a close eye on your baby to check for any allergic reactions. These usually appear quickly, within a few minutes of your baby eating something they shouldn't, so if you spot any of the following symptoms soon after eating, seek medical attention:

- Sneezing
- Red, itchy, watery eyes
- Red, itchy rash
- Hives around their mouth
- Swollen lips or tongue
- Wheezing and coughing
- A suddenly runny or blocked nose
- Worsening asthma or eczema

Alternatively, your baby may have a food intolerance, where their tummy struggles to digest certain foods. Though less serious than a food allergy, intolerances can still be uncomfortable for your little one, bringing problems of their own which shouldn't be ignored.

Unlike allergic reactions, which generally come on very quickly, food intolerance symptoms usually appear a few hours after eating a certain food, and include:

- Tummy ache
- Diarrhoea
- Gassiness/wind

Fortunately, most food intolerances can be managed through simple dietary changes, but speak to your doctor if you are at all worried so that they can advise on the best course of action.

Life as an allergen dad
(Mike's story)

Like us, chances are you'll discover your little one has an allergy completely by chance. We found out our eldest was dairy anaphylactic when we began weaning. A mouthful of baby porridge at six months turned into a frantic dash to the hospital.

As soon as the porridge hit her lips, she developed hives around her mouth, followed by a swollen tongue and lips. We had no idea what was happening, but we knew it was serious.

On arrival, the nurses identified straight away that she was having an anaphylactic reaction, giving her adrenaline, steroids and antihistamine. It was a complete shock.

Neither my wife nor I have allergies, and allergen awareness was pretty much non-existent at the time. I'd heard of people having life-threatening reactions to peanuts but had no idea that dairy could cause the same thing. But the doctor confirmed our daughter was dairy anaphylactic, meaning she'd have to carry an EpiPen and antihistamine with her at all times. We were advised to expose her to the 14 major allergens, which confirmed she also had egg anaphylaxis. We made the decision to remove dairy and egg from our diets and nothing that contained either ingredient entered our house.

Since then, our daughter had multiple skin prick tests and blood tests to determine the severity of her allergies, while our local allergy clinic helped us develop a specialist plan on how best to move forward. We embarked on a dairy and egg "ladder", which basically exposed our daughter to her allergens at varied strengths. This had some success. We now know she can tolerate both allergens in small doses under certain circumstances, such as in biscuits. However, ten years later, she is still anaphylactic, and her allergies will be with her for the rest of her life.

Fortunately, allergen awareness has improved significantly over recent years, while the availability of allergy-friendly foods has drastically improved, taking away some of the worry.

But, as your children get older, you can't be with them every moment of every day to make sure they're safe. There are times when you have to entrust your child's health and safety to others. This can cause anxiety, so I want to highlight some of these scenarios and how we manage them:

Childcare and school – Keep communicating with the nursery/school and be assertive. Make sure they know about your kid's allergies, what to look out for if they have a reaction and how to manage it. Work with them to develop an allergy plan, printed out so that it stays with your child, and ensure the school has their own allergy kit. You might have to provide your own milk alternatives or packed lunches if the school cannot provide safe meals for your child to eat. But, for your child's social well-being, I'd suggest not separating them from others during mealtimes. You don't want their school experience to be defined by their allergies.

Playdates and parties – If your kid goes to a friend's house, always chat with the parents beforehand. Ask what they plan to cook and check the ingredient lists to make sure the food is safe. Ensure your child has their allergy medication with them and chat with the parents about how to use it. Attend the parties yourself if you're at all worried.

Holidays – Research possible holiday destinations in terms of their allergy awareness and food availability. Some places are better than others. For ease, we typically take lots of food away with us, as the prices of allergy-friendly foods are usually very high abroad. If you're flying, take your medication through security, ideally with a doctor's note, to avoid any issues getting things through. In advance and when on the plane, make the cabin crew aware of your allergies (yup, we're the family that means you sometimes can't eat nuts on planes!).

Raising a kid with allergies is difficult and challenging, especially in the early stages when you are new to this world. But the more you go through life, the easier it becomes. The key is to try and lead as "normal" a life as possible. Don't avoid doing things for fear of something going wrong. Chances are, it will all be fine. The hardest part is dealing with your own anxiety. Manage that and half the battle is won.

Mike left his career in the NHS to take on a much more challenging role... stay-at-home dad of four. Mike and his family live in North Wales and you can follow their escapades on Instagram @daddy_freckle.

Avoiding fussy eaters

A child's relationship with food is closely linked to their eating experiences during these formative early years. The more diverse the taste experiences you expose them to, and the more you can make mealtimes enjoyable, interesting and stress-free from the start, the more open they should be to trying new things as they get older.

It should be noted that while fussiness isn't genetic, there may be certain personality traits in your child that make them more prone to fussy eating. Perhaps they're extremely headstrong or get anxious easily, which can make mealtimes more of a challenge. Plus, it's totally normal for toddlers to go through stages of fussy eating, or to love a certain food one day and then completely reject it the next. That doesn't necessarily mean they don't like it or won't eat it in future, so don't cross it off the menu permanently.

Whatever obstacles you face, try these do's and don'ts to give your child and their relationship with food the best possible start.

DO

Keep things interesting

When you're short on time and patience, it's easy to fall into a routine of giving your baby or toddler the same limited selection of dishes you know for sure they like and will eat. But this won't do them any favours in the long run. Try to mix things up, incorporate something new into every meal (even if just on the side), serve the same food in different ways (for example, tomato sauce instead of raw tomato) and inject some fun into mealtimes by experimenting with different colours and shapes on their plate.

Eat together

Eating together as a family is one of the best things you can do to encourage your toddler to be a good eater. Not only is it a real time saver (being able to cook just one thing for everyone), but family mealtimes are also great bonding experiences that help kids develop important conversational, social and motor skills that will set them up for life.

Stay positive

Don't project your personal hang-ups or food dislikes onto your child. Talk positively about food at every opportunity. Say everything is yummy, even if you don't like it yourself. Anything you can do to avoid negative language and make mealtimes a positive experience will pay dividends for years to come.

Play the long game

Track what they're eating over the course of a day and the whole week, rather than getting too hung up on one bad mealtime. If they don't eat much at lunch, they'll almost certainly make up for it later in the day. Equally, they may have a bad day but get plenty to eat over the course of the week.

DON'T

Overwhelm them

Don't overwhelm them with large portions. Start them off with small amounts of food on their plate. They can always ask for more if they like it.

Force them

When a child feels pressured to eat, it will almost always lead to tantrums, tears and untouched plates. Never force food into their mouths or make them eat something if they really don't want to. It's far better to save an uneaten meal for later, try again another day or just eat it yourself and make a big show of how delicious it is.

Resort to threats and bribery

Don't make threats to get them to finish their plate if they don't want to. This can lead to food refusal, which can make them anxious about mealtimes. The same applies to bribes, which can lead to them expecting incentives every time they finish a meal.

Surprise them

Tell them what you're making before you start cooking, or better yet, involve them in preparing their food. This will allow them time to prepare mentally for a meal while giving them ownership and control over what they're eating, avoiding food anxiety.

Give up

If you feed your little one a new type of food and they reject it, that doesn't necessarily mean they don't like what you're giving them. It could just be that they don't fancy it at that moment, or they need a nappy change, or they're tired. If they do turn their nose up, try giving them the same thing again the next day, or at a different time of day. It can take five to ten tastes for a baby to accept a new food, so don't give up.

> ## DADVICE
>
> Unless your kid has specific allergies, try not to get in the habit of cooking separate meals for them when you are eating together as a family. If you can get to a point where your kid eats what the adults eat (just with less seasoning), you'll save yourself years of time, effort and waste.

CHAPTER 6

WILL I EVER SLEEP AGAIN?

You'll be pleased to hear that the answer to this question is, most definitely, yes. Your Sunday morning lie-ins are not lost forever. And there will be a time (in the not-too-distant future) when your baby will learn to sleep through the night. Because they all do eventually. Hence why you rarely hear of adults who wake up crying multiple times during the night, demanding a nappy change and a warm cup of milk.

But there's no denying that the early months of parenthood are seriously tough. Sleep, or your lack of it, will consume most of your daily thoughts and conversations. Everyone you see will ask if you're getting any. You'll compete with your partner over who's had less of it. And you'll find yourself walking around in a zombie-like trance, dreaming of the day when your baby will sleep for more than a couple of hours at a time.

As you'll have gathered by now, no two babies are alike. The amount they sleep will depend on how old they are, whether they were born prematurely, their weight and how well they feed. External factors will have a bearing too, from where they're sleeping and in what position, to what they're wearing, and the light, sound and temperature levels of their sleeping environment.

And when it comes to their sleeping patterns and establishing a routine, it can be something of a lottery. What works for one baby won't necessarily work for another. You'll almost certainly need to try a few different approaches before you find what works for your baby. My advice for you is to give each one a proper go before moving on to the next. As a general rule, you should only consider a routine to be established once your baby has followed the same pattern consistently for seven days in a row. So, even if you don't see immediate results, stick at it, stay strong and, above all, be consistent.

It really is a minefield. But this chapter will give you all the practical advice you need to navigate through it in one piece.

Too Tired

Too tired to wash.
Too tired to function.
Too knackered to see past
this new baby junction.

Too tired to read.
Too tired to write.
Just dreaming that one day
they'll sleep through the night.

Too tired to cook.
Too tired to eat.
When life is just swaddle,
shush, pat on repeat.

Too tired to iron.
Too tired to clean.
Two sunken black holes where
my eyes once had been.

Too tired to listen.
Too tired to speak.
No clue how we'll possibly
get through the week.

Too tired to work.
Too tired to think.
This zonked zombie life has
me right on the brink.

Too tired to argue.
Too tired to fight.
Tiptoeing around, scared
to turn on the light.

Too tired to hug.
Too tired to kiss.
With sleep so damn precious,
we'll give sex a miss.

Too tired to laugh.
Too tired to cry.
Just so fucking tired I
think I might die.

BONUS VERSE FOR
FIRST-TIME PARENTS

It will all be okay.
Don't worry. Don't fret.
This sleep-deprived state,
is one we all get.
While it seems never-ending,
(and feels proper shite),
it's a phase. It will pass.
So, good luck and sleep tight.

How much sleep does my baby need?

Newborn to 3 months – In the first few months of your baby's life, they should sleep for between 14 and 17 hours every day. Unfortunately, this isn't all in one go but rather spread out over each 24-hour period in a series of short power naps. The length of these naps will vary depending on your baby, but they usually range from 45 minutes to a couple of hours at a time. For new parents, this is by far the hardest phase, as the months of broken sleep take their toll.

Adding to your woes, most newborns experience day/night confusion, which means they sleep more during the day than they do at night. As adults, we have an internal body clock known as the circadian rhythm, which wakes us up in the morning and makes us sleepy at night. Newborns don't have this, and it can take around three to four months before their internal body clock gets into step with ours.

> ## DADVICE
>
> Take your baby outside during the day to get some fresh air and natural light. Studies have shown that babies who are exposed to natural light during the day sleep better at night and adapt faster to the 24-hour circadian rhythm. Similarly, allow lots of natural light into their sleeping environment for daytime naps and save complete darkness (using curtains or blackout blinds) for the night.

4 to 12 months – For the rest of your baby's first year, they should sleep for around 12–16 hours per day. As soon as their circadian rhythm kicks in, you should notice they are more alert and have shorter naps during daylight hours, while their sleeps at night gradually get longer.

1 to 2 years – Your baby/toddler will likely still have a nap or possibly two during the day, though most of their rest will be at night, totalling between 11 and 14 hours per day. At this stage, they will be learning a lot, so proper rest is needed to let their brain and body recharge.

3 years – Your toddler should be getting around 10–13 hours each day. They may still need one short nap during the day, particularly if they are cranky in the afternoons or can't keep their eyes open come dinner time.

Settling your baby

Putting your baby down to sleep can feel a bit like you're handling a ticking time bomb. Do it wrong and BOOM... they're wide awake, crying and unsettled, meaning you have to start the whole settling process again from scratch.

Knowing when to put your baby down for a nap is the first challenge. Lay them down too early, and you risk them getting in a tizzy and not going to sleep. Leave it too late and they may be overtired, leading to more waterworks. The key is knowing your baby's sleep signals and acting on them quickly. The most common ones include:

- Yawning
- A glazed look and laboured blinking
- Change in temperament (from loud to quiet or calm to agitated)
- Rubbing their eyes or pulling their ears or hair
- Arching backwards
- Altered cry (usually more of a moaning sound)
- Snuggling into you when being held

When you spot any of these sleepy signals, calmly prepare your baby for bed (wrapping them in a swaddle or putting them in a sleeping bag, singing them a lullaby or putting on some white noise) and gently lay them down.

DID YOU KNOW?

Babies have been found to respond positively to white noise – effectively a "shh" sound like waves or a vacuum cleaner – which can calm them and help them go to sleep. There are lots of different white noise sleeping aids you can buy that play this or similar repetitive sounds, like a mother's heartbeat in the womb, which you can start using from birth as your baby falls asleep. Over time, they should start to associate these sounds with nap time, helping them settle.

Try to get in the habit of changing your baby's nappy before they are due a nap, as this can often make the process of settling them easier. A nappy change can be quite a big ordeal, with your baby getting partially naked and therefore cold, or requiring a change of clothes, which can jolt them out of their sleepy state.

DADVICE

While you can rock your baby in your arms and wait for them to fall asleep before putting them down, for daytime naps, try to lay them in their Moses basket or cot while they are still awake. By doing this, they will learn how to settle themselves to sleep rather than always relying on you to do it.

During the night, however, you want to minimize the amount of time they are awake between feeds and wake-ups, so getting them to fall asleep in your arms before laying them down is fine.

Putting your baby down right

If your newborn wakes up or cries every time you put them down to sleep, try one of these three settling techniques:

Bottom-first

It might seem most natural to gently lower your baby into their cot headfirst, letting their head rest on the mattress before their shoulders, back and bottom. However, this can trigger a baby's startle reflex, jolting them awake. Instead, try putting them down the opposite way... first their bum, before gently rolling them down onto their back with their head touching down last.

Containment hold

Holding your baby close into your body, bend down all the way to their mattress so they are in contact with you the whole time. As you slowly pull your body away, leave one hand on the crown of their head and the other resting gently on their tummy or chest. This helps your baby feel secure as their connection to you is never broken.

Leave your hands in place for as long as it takes your baby to settle, then gradually remove your hand from their head, waiting a little longer before slowly taking your hand off their tummy. If they fuss, reconnect by placing your hand back onto their tummy until they settle again.

The magic "shush-pat"

This settling technique, suggested for babies under six months old, can be highly effective during the nights in getting a fully-fed baby back to sleep after they wake up for no apparent reason.

Hold your crying baby close to your chest in an upright position while doing these three actions at the same time:

- Make long, reasonably loud shushing sounds (a bit like a fast-running tap).
- Firmly and rhythmically pat your baby in the centre of their back.
- Gently bounce up and down, bending your knees to create the bouncing motion.

The theory behind this is that babies' brains can only process two things at a time, so by shushing, patting and bouncing in unison, you are giving them too many things to think about, and they dutifully fall asleep.

Once your baby has stopped crying, continue doing the three shush-pat actions for around ten minutes before slowing down your patting rhythm and bouncing as you gradually decrease the volume of your shushing, before stopping altogether and laying them down. If your baby wakes up crying soon after, pick them up again and restart the process.

Consistency and perseverance are key with this technique. It may take some time for them to find comfort in this method, but once they do, any combination of shushing, patting or bouncing – whether in your arms or while lying down – will become a mental cue for them to fall soundly asleep.

Why isn't my baby sleeping?
A troubleshooting guide

Babies need a lot of sleep for their physical and cognitive development, so they should naturally get the right amount for their age. However, if your baby is waking up crying, unhappy or unrested, it's usually because something's wrong.

The top reasons your baby may be waking up prematurely are:

Too hot or cold

The temperature of the room where your baby is sleeping and the amount of clothes they're wearing are fundamental to ensuring they have quality sleep. While this can be difficult to manage in the depths of winter and the heights of summer, you should try to maintain your baby's room at 16–20°C (60–68°F). If your baby's nursery doesn't have its own built-in climate controls, it's worth investing in a room thermometer, heater and fan (ensuring they don't point directly at your baby's cot while they are sleeping).

Check it		Fix it
If your baby is waking up with wet hair, damp clothes or a sweaty chest or back, either the room is too hot or they are wearing too many layers.	$\longrightarrow$	Remove a layer of clothing, use a lighter-weight covering or sleeping bag and put a fan into their room to bring the temperature down.
If your baby is restless during naps or you find them sleeping on their hands or in the corner of the cot, these are signs they might be too cold.	$\longrightarrow$	Make sure they are wearing a vest under their sleepsuit, add socks if they have bare feet and tuck in an extra blanket over them when they sleep. If you're using a sleeping bag, buy a thicker one ("higher tog") for the winter months.

Layering up for naps and night-time sleeps

When your baby starts rolling over or crawling, it's a lot harder to keep them warm during the night as they are prone to wriggling out of their swaddles or covers. If you haven't already, this is usually your sign to switch to sleeping bags during their naps and night-time sleeps.

To cover you for varying temperatures throughout the year, invest in a few different sleeping bags of different thickness or "tog". Tog 1 is the lightest, which is best for the summer and hot climates; Tog 2 is a bit thicker and a good all-rounder, while Tog 3 is the thickest and best for the cold winter months. The clothes you put your baby in are also important and should be adjusted depending on the room temperature and sleeping bag tog you're using.

As a general rule, it's better for your baby to be too cool rather than too hot. And don't worry if their extremities (face, hands and feet) feel cool to touch during the winter months, so long as the rest of them is warm.

Nursery Temperature

24°C (75.2°F) or over	TOG 1	
22°C (71.6°F)	TOG 1	
20°C (68°F)	TOG 2	
18°C (64.4°F)	TOG 2	
16°C (60.8°F) or under	TOG 3	

They're wet

While most nappies are designed to manage a baby's natural evacuations, wicking them away from their body to minimize discomfort, a big pee or poo can still make a baby uncomfortable enough to wake them up.

Check it

Check your baby's nappy for excessive moisture or a poo and feel their clothes, sleeping bag and mattress in case they've had a leak.

→

Fix it

Always put your little one down to sleep with a clean, dry nappy. For night-times, put your baby in a special heavy-duty nappy that absorbs more liquid, as this will encourage longer sleeps during the night without needing to change them every few hours. **This is especially important if you are using reusable nappies.**

Congested

As their immune systems are still developing, babies are especially prone to catching coughs, colds and other bugs. These can prove hard to shift and will disrupt your baby's sleep cycle.

Check it

If your baby has a persistent cough or a blocked or runny nose, you may find they struggle to fall into a deep sleep and wake up more regularly throughout the night.

→

Fix it

Clear their airways as best as you can before putting them down to sleep, using saline drops to help wash away built-up mucus. From two months old, you can also put a diffuser or plug-in humidifier with vapour oil in their room to help them breathe more easily.

Listen to your baby's breathing during their nap. If they are snoring or mouth breathing, but don't have other symptoms of a cold, this can be a sign of allergies or sleep apnoea, which need to get checked by a doctor.

→

Film a video of your baby making these noises while they are asleep and show it to your doctor, to help them give a more accurate diagnosis.

In pain

There are certain things to look out for which indicate a baby could be in pain and some intervention is needed.

Check it		Fix it
If your baby is still crying despite being comforted, changed and fed, this could be a sign of colic or teething.	⟶	Check your baby's gums for teeth cutting through and (if over two months old) give them liquid paracetamol half an hour before they go to sleep.
Excessive night waking every 30 minutes to an hour could signal reflux, tongue tie or allergies.	⟶	Burp your baby for longer than usual, to make sure any excess gas has been released.
If your baby is arching their back and only comfortable sleeping upright on you, this could indicate colic, reflux or excess gas.	⟶	Let your baby have more upright sleeps on you or in a carrier, to ensure they get some quality sleep during the day.

Startled and distracted

It's common for babies to flail their arms and legs around during a sleep – known as the "startle reflex" – which can make them wake up. While they should go back to sleep on their own, sometimes other factors might be preventing them from settling.

Check it		Fix it
Watch your baby closely during their naps to see when their "startle reflex" kicks in (usually soon after falling asleep) and how well they settle afterwards.	⟶	Under the age of four months, swaddling is most effective at minimizing the startle reflex (see page 98). Shush your baby or put a calming hand on their head or chest when they startle themselves awake. The quicker you respond, the more likely they are to fall back asleep.
If they look around rather than close their eyes and drift back to sleep, there may be too much visual stimulation in their room.	⟶	Remove distractions like baby mobiles and cuddly toys from their sleeping area. Put on white noise to help soothe them back to sleep.

Hungry

This is by far the hardest reason to diagnose, especially if your partner is breastfeeding, as it's difficult to know exactly how much your baby is drinking at each feed. Generally, a well-fed baby should look relaxed and satisfied after a feed (i.e. not crying out for more), and enjoy a minimum of 45 minutes of quality sleep after each one. If this isn't the case, a change of approach may be needed.

Check it	Fix it
Refer to the milestones checklist on page 212 to see if your baby is due their next growth spurt or developmental leap. If so, it's likely that their sleeping patterns will be disrupted and they will need more regular feeds than usual.	Encourage your baby to take longer feeds on the breast or try cluster feeding (see page 180) before they go down to sleep.
If, from three months old, your baby still isn't sleeping for longer stints during the night (and you've discounted all the other potential causes listed earlier), chances are their rumbling tummy may be waking them up prematurely.	Try implementing a "dream feed" (see pages 180–1), to top them up with milk before you go to bed. And don't forget that external factors could be to blame. For example, in hotter weather, your baby might need more to drink than usual before they are satisfied.
If your baby has recently been sick or suffers from reflux, it's likely they will be hungry sooner between feeds, affecting their sleep.	Try feeding your baby in a more upright position, burping them both during and after a feed, and waiting for longer after a feed before putting them down to sleep.

DADVICE

If you're worried that your baby still isn't getting enough to drink, try bottle feeding using expressed milk, so you can more accurately track how much they are drinking at each feed.

And, if all else fails, consider switching to formula for some or all of your feeds (if you haven't already), as this can be more filling and therefore promote longer sleeps.

Establishing a routine

Nothing can prepare you for the extreme levels of sleep deprivation you'll experience during the first few weeks and months of your baby's life. With your baby feeding on-demand and only sleeping for an hour or two at a time, this gruelling 24-hour schedule makes zombies of us all.

Well-intentioned family members will tell you and your partner to "sleep when the baby sleeps". As great as this sounds, unfortunately it's rarely possible in practice. In the brief windows when your baby is asleep, you'll have countless other things that need doing such as eating, showering, laundry and dealing with visitors, meaning sleep often gets sacrificed.

At some point, though, most parents realize that operating with so little sleep is not sustainable in the long term, and the only solution is to get the baby into some kind of routine.

There are no quick fixes here. A routine can take weeks, even months, of hard work, consistency, teamwork and patience to establish. But it's worth the effort to win back some time for yourselves and get the rest you need to function properly.

DID YOU KNOW?

Silence isn't always golden. If you always tiptoe around the house whenever your baby goes for a nap, you may be subconsciously training them to only be able to sleep in absolute silence. Whereas if you worry a little less about normal household noises, whether hoovering outside their room, doing the dishes or watching TV next door, they are more likely to be able to sleep with some background noise, while learning to settle themselves should anything wake them up.

"It's amazing that you can be that exhausted and that happy at the same time."

Ryan Reynolds

When to start

Babies are quick learners, and they generally love the structure of a routine. Knowing when they are going to be fed and when they are going to sleep can be a real comfort to them, reducing anxiety while aiding better sleep (for them and for you).

For the first month of your baby's life, it's recommended that you feed on-demand. However, from four weeks onwards, you can start to take more control of your baby's feeding and sleeping schedule, to give some structure to your day and start laying the foundations for a more consistent routine as your baby gets older.

Creating sleep cues for your baby

Sleep cues are physical actions, sounds or objects that signal to your baby that it is time to go to sleep. They include:

- Putting on white noise.
- Singing a certain song or playing a specific piece of music.
- Giving your baby a special comforter or favourite teddy (though it's recommended for babies under 12 months that this be removed from their bed after they fall asleep).
- Swaddling or putting them in a sleeping bag.

Consistency and repetition are key here. If you use the same sleep cues before every nap, your baby will quickly learn what they mean, mentally preparing them for sleep.

Starting a bedtime ritual

The same logic applies to creating a bedtime ritual for your baby, to let them know when the day is over and prepare them for longer night-time sleeps. Unlike the regular sleep cues which you should do before every nap, the bedtime ritual is a once-a-day event, done at roughly the same time and in the same way every evening. This might include:

- Creating a calm environment at home half an hour before your chosen bedtime, dimming lights and minimizing potential distractions for your baby.
- Giving your baby a warm bath.
- Practising some baby massage (using a baby oil or lotion to massage your baby's legs and arms gently, focusing most on their ankles, wrists and fingers).
- Putting on a fresh nappy and their bedtime clothes.
- Reading them a bedtime story or singing a favourite lullaby.
- Closing the curtains or blinds.
- Giving them their final feed in a dimly lit room before using your other daytime sleep cues (swaddle/comforter/white noise).

DADVICE

If you can, set your baby's new bedtime at a time when both you and your partner will be at home. Not only is it a great bonding opportunity for you, but it's also beneficial for your baby to experience both parents putting them to bed – both together and individually – so that they don't become overly dependent on just one parent at bedtime.

The easiest routine for first-time parents

DADVICE

There are countless different routines you can try – from strict schedules involving precise timings and lengths of activities to more flexible, relaxed alternatives – each with its own book to read and digest before putting them into practice. However, in my experience, the easiest to follow, and the one us dads can get most involved in, is "The EASY Method" by Tracy Hogg, which I recommend above all others.

Unlike some of the super strict routines out there, which try to get your baby to do certain things at certain times, the EASY Method is much more flexible, focused instead on the order that you and your baby do certain activities throughout the day.

The EASY Method is a recurring process that involves eating, playing and resting, in that order:

E is for Eating – When your baby wakes up from their nap, feed them right away until they have had their fill. Though small babies will often want to fall back to sleep straight after a feed, do whatever you can to keep them awake for the next crucial part of this routine.

A is for Activity – Do an activity with your baby until it's time for their nap. This could be changing their nappy, playing with them on a playmat, singing them a song or reading to them.

S is for Sleep – When they start to show signs that they are tired, put them down in their cot and settle them to sleep.

Y is for You Time – Once they're down, this is your time to use however you like – have yourself a little nap, put your feet up, watch a boxset or catch up on life admin until your baby wakes up and you start the EASY routine again.

One of the main aims of this method is to keep your baby stimulated and engaged after a feed (in the hopes of tiring them out) while training them not to "feed to sleep" during the daylight hours.

In the evening, from 7 p.m. to 7 a.m., when you want your baby to sleep as long as possible so you and your partner can get a proper rest, the EASY Method changes slightly.

It recommends that for the last EASY sequence of the day before your baby's official bedtime, you should do a "cluster feed" to fill them up for the night and discourage premature wake-ups. This means feeding your baby once between 5 and 7 p.m., doing a very calm last activity of the day (giving them a bath is ideal), then *feeding them once more* before putting them down to sleep.

Then, at around 10 p.m., carefully pick your baby up and offer them a feed (breast or bottle) *while they are still asleep* – known as a "dream feed". This top-up of milk should encourage them to sleep for longer stints during the night (four hours or more in some cases), allowing you to get more sleep too.

During the rest of the night, skip the A/Activity part of the routine (apart from any nappy changes that might be required), as you don't want to wake the baby more than you have to during the early hours. Just focus on feeding, avoiding distractions, before settling your baby back to sleep.

Then, when morning arrives, you restart the EASY Method once again, repeating the four steps in order until bedtime comes around again.

In a matter of weeks, you should start to see progress and some consistency emerging in your baby's daily routine, while the length of their night-time sleeps should also stretch out.

TOP TIPS

To get the most out of the EASY Method

- Don't panic if you don't see immediate results. It takes time for any new routine to bed in, and it may take a few weeks before you get any quality "you time".

- Physically write down your EASY schedule, noting the time of each feed, the length of each sleep and what activity you do in between. Look back at your old notes and judge success on the small improvements you see week by week rather than day by day.

- Do the dream feed yourself if you can – it's not only a great bonding experience for you, but it will also allow your partner to go straight to bed after the last cluster feed, at around 7 p.m., giving her a decent run of restorative, uninterrupted sleep every night.

- The dream feed doesn't suit all babies, so don't force it. Try the technique for three or four nights, and if your baby isn't sleeping for longer stretches after each dream feed, or wakes up/won't go down again afterwards, abandon it altogether.

Sleep training

If your baby is fighting sleep every time you put them down or struggles to self-soothe (i.e. fall asleep by themselves), you may want to give sleep training a go. This involves being stricter with how you engage with your baby after they've been put down for a sleep, to help them get comfortable self-soothing and sleeping on their own.

Sleep training is not appropriate for very young babies. Their bodies are still adjusting to natural sleep cycles, and they thrive on cuddles and the comfort and security of having you nearby. Most healthcare professionals recommend waiting until your baby is around six months old, when their sleep patterns are more established, before starting sleep training (though some parents do decide to start a bit earlier).

There are four main techniques you can try. Which you choose comes down to personal preference:

The cry it out method

Settle your baby, put them down awake in their cot and say "night night" before leaving the room. If they start crying, don't go back in to soothe them straight away. Wait outside the door and see if they calm down by themselves. If ten minutes go by and they're still crying, go back in, settle them again (checking they don't need a nappy change and aren't in pain), before trying this process again.

DADVICE

This can be a really difficult process for parents, as nobody likes to hear their baby in distress. But, as long as there is no specific reason for their crying that needs attention, leaving them to cry won't cause any lasting damage to your baby or your relationship. Lots of parents also like this method as it usually has the quickest results.

The Ferber method

This is similar to the cry it out method, but rather than leaving your baby alone for ten minutes to figure things out for themselves, instead, you *gradually increase* the amount of time you wait before going back into their room to help them settle.

For the first few nights, you can go back into their room as soon as they start crying after being put down. But, over time, gradually delay your response time by one-minute increments (up to a maximum of ten minutes) to help your baby learn to self-soothe.

The check and console method

This method helps reassure your baby that you are there for them and they have nothing to fear from going to sleep. Whether your baby is crying or not, go into their room every few minutes to check on them, giving them a gentle stroke or pat to reassure them.

Over the course of a month, gradually increase the gaps between these check-ins until they are about 15 minutes apart. If you find your baby waking up or getting over-excited during these nightly check-ins, decrease their regularity.

The chair method

With this method, settle your baby as usual and put them down drowsy but still awake. Stay by the side of their cot to offer a reassuring word if they need it, but don't touch them or pick them up.

Every night, gradually move further away from their cot while verbally soothing them, if needed, or sit down in a chair nearby while you wait for them to fall asleep. In a couple of weeks, most babies will teach themselves to self-soothe using this method.

DID YOU KNOW?

Most cots allow you to adjust the mattress height as your baby grows. When your baby is small and doesn't move or roll over during a sleep, it's best to have the cot mattress at its highest setting to save your back.

But, as soon as your baby is strong enough to lift themselves up and can get into a sitting position on their own, this is your sign to move the mattress down to discourage them from climbing out and hurting themselves.

Sleep vs sex

When you're navigating life with a newborn, sex may well be the last thing on your mind. But there will come a time when sleep isn't the only thing you crave. It's usually us dads who are the first to suggest it. But don't be surprised if your partner doesn't share your enthusiasm – it may take some time for her to feel ready for sex again.

Let's take a look at some of the reasons why she might be feeling this way, and what you can do to get the physical side of your relationship back on track.

She's exhausted

Tiredness kills sex drives, and nobody is more tired than a new mum. Looking after a newborn is exhausting work, so if she has the choice between sex and sleep, the latter is going to win every time.

If you want to help your partner get her mojo back, more sleep is usually the best solution. This means earlier to bed, more support from you at home and working together to get your baby into a routine that gets them sleeping through the night.

She's worried it will hurt

Lots of new mums experience a very natural fear that sex will hurt or be uncomfortable. She may have stitches that need time to heal, or swelling and discomfort in and around her vagina, so wait until after your partner's six-week check-up when she hopefully gets the all-clear. Even then, she might still be apprehensive, depending on how smoothly her postpartum recovery is going.

When she does feel ready, take things slowly and stop if she feels any kind of discomfort. And remember, there are plenty of other ways to be intimate with each other.

She feels "touched out"

In the early days of motherhood, your partner will have the baby physically in her arms for the vast majority of the day, feeding off her, sleeping on her and nestling into her, to the point where she may become irritable, overwhelmed and dread the thought of any further physical contact.

Feeling "touched out" is very common in new mums, so don't take it personally. Give your partner the space she needs, offer to take the baby to give her a physical break from them, and don't put any pressure on her to be intimate until she's ready.

She feels insecure

The process of pregnancy and birth changes a woman's body. Your partner might have stretch marks, sagging skin, varicose veins or physical scars that make her feel self-conscious, vulnerable and insecure about being naked in front of you.

Show her that none of these changes affect how you see her. Tell her she's beautiful. Tell her you love her stretch marks and reassure her that her body is sexy. Because it bears the marks of motherhood, that just means you love it, and her, even more.

She needs to feel loved

When you're both so busy getting to grips with parenthood and looking after your baby, it can feel a bit like you're flatmates rather than loving partners. Though that intimate connection won't be gone for good, it can take some time to build back.

Make sure your partner feels loved and appreciated and give her time to warm up to the idea of sex. Spend as much quality time together as you can. Ask her how she's feeling and if there's anything she needs from you. That way, she'll feel much more like your partner rather than just the woman who looks after your baby.

DADVICE

A word of warning about sex during the first few months of parenthood. It's a common belief that new mums cannot get pregnant again while breastfeeding or before their period has returned after childbirth. As many parents have found out to their surprise, this isn't always the case. So, if you want to avoid having two babies in quick succession, it's best to play it extra safe (if you know what I mean)!

Moving your baby into their own bedroom

As you'll have picked up by now, it's recommended that your baby sleeps in the same room as you until they are around six months old. Depending on how well your baby is sleeping and how comfortable you are with this arrangement, some parents choose to make this separation earlier.

This can be quite a big transition for babies, leading to difficulty settling or interrupted sleep cycles, but there are lots of things you can do to prepare them for this switch.

Nursery naps – Once your baby's nursery is set up, start giving them one of their daytime naps in their new room before increasing the regularity until they have all daytime naps in there. This will get them comfortable in their nursery and make them associate it with sleeping.

Familiarization – Talk to them about their room, show them around and spend some quality time in there together, so they know the space well before it becomes their mainstay.

New cot – If you are also transitioning your baby into a new cot as part of the move, let them spend some quality time in their new bed during the day. Allow them to have some independent play in there with their favourite toys, so that it becomes a safe and familiar space for them.

Bedtime ritual – Make your baby's nursery a key part of their bedtime routine, doing as many of your chosen sleep cues in their room before putting them down to sleep in yours.

Be consistent – Once you've decided to move your baby into their new room, make the transition and stick with it. Even if they struggle to adapt right away, don't give up and move them back into your room, as this will only cause confusion.

At the end of the day, you want your baby to love their bedroom. Any positive association you can build will not only help them enjoy better sleep in the room, but it will also become a safe space where they can play and relax once they start sitting up and moving around.

What to do when your baby stops napping

Once your baby is in an established routine, they will usually have around two to three naps per day, of varying lengths depending on their sleep preferences. One nap should soon emerge as their favourite, where they sleep the best and longest, accompanied by one or two shorter naps on either side.

As your baby approaches their first birthday, it's normal that they will become fussier during their shorter daytime naps, either refusing to go to sleep or crying for longer before drifting off. This is usually a sign that your baby is ready to drop a nap. Generally, sometime between 12 and 24 months, most babies will settle into having just one nap a day.

This change can be quite a blow for parents, as you suddenly lose key chunks of free time that you had to yourself during the day. Of course, there are positives too, such as not being so restricted or tied down at home, meaning you can leave the house, see friends, or just get on with things without worrying about waking the baby.

There will come a time, though – usually when your child is between two and three years old – when they will stop sleeping during the day entirely. No more naps, just straight through from breakfast to bath-time. As much as this thought may fill you with dread, don't fret. There are lots of things you can do to maintain some balance in your parenting workload while giving you and your child the downtime you both need.

Top-up naps

When your little one starts dropping their only remaining daytime nap, that doesn't mean they're done with napping entirely. Try offering them a nap every other day, or twice a week instead, as they may well still need a top-up.

Head out

If they stop napping in their cot, try taking them for a walk in the pram or a drive in the car. If they're genuinely tired, they'll usually fall asleep, giving you a little extra time to yourself.

Implement quiet time

While your little one may not want to sleep, that doesn't mean they wouldn't benefit from a little downtime. Implementing chill time – just for an hour or two after lunch – is a great way for everyone to get some rest while breaking up what is a long day of parenting.

For younger children, this could be lying on the bed reading stories or listening to an audiobook together, or just doing some calm activities like colouring or a puzzle. As they get older, stick them in front of a film or, better yet, join them on the sofa and have yourself a little nap.

Earlier bedtime

When your child drops their final nap, this can lead to them becoming seriously overtired by the time their bedtime comes around, making the witching hour (usually between 5 and 6 p.m., when everyone is knackered and patience is running low) even more challenging than it needs to be.

Rather than sticking religiously to your old end-of-day routine, bring forward their bedtime by an hour or so after that final nap has been officially dropped. Once they get more accustomed to going all day without a nap, and you notice their energy levels being more consistent throughout the day, you can gradually move back their bedtime to whatever time suits you best.

"WHY DO KIDS NOT UNDERSTAND THEIR NAP IS NOT FOR THEM, BUT FOR US?"

Alyson Hannigan

Transition from cot to bed

Every baby has a different relationship with their cot. Some are snugglers who love the comfort and security of their own enclosed space. Others are adventurers who like to climb and explore, and can't be contained. But there will come a time in every toddler's life when their natural curiosity gets the better of them and they can no longer be confined.

Once your toddler develops this adventurous streak and you catch them trying to climb out of their cot (whether successfully or not), for their own safety, it's time to make the big transition from cot to bed. If your cot has removable sides, you can simply take out one panel so your toddler can get in and out easily without needing to climb the bars. If not, you can either move them into a special low-slung toddler bed or skip this stage and put them in a standard single bed. Just be prepared that you may need to attach temporary side supports to prevent them from rolling out of bed in their sleep.

Either way, prepare yourself for some unusual nap and night-time activity, as your toddler tests the boundaries of their newfound freedom. Common behaviours you'll notice include:

- Repeatedly getting out of bed to play and explore their bedroom.
- Escaping their room to find you.
- Turning on the main light or looking out the window.
- Taking longer to go to sleep.
- Coming into your room and/or bed in the middle of the night.
- Falling/rolling out of bed.
- Sleeping on the floor of their room.
- Waking up earlier than usual in the morning and staying up later at night.

All these behaviours are entirely normal and should settle down after a few weeks (a couple of months at most) once they've got used to the new set-up. But there are certain things you can do to make the transition a little easier for everyone…

- When first changing their sleeping arrangements, avoid saying phrases like "stay in bed" and "don't get out of bed". There's a chance they never even considered they had a choice in the matter, so don't plant the idea in their head prematurely. Of course, as they get older, these will become your nightly catchphrases... but try to avoid them at the outset.

- Install a nursery camera in your child's room so you can keep an eye on their movements from afar. If they can see you watching from the door, they're more likely to get out of bed and engage with you.

- Let them explore their room after you put them down (if they want to). However, if they're spending ages out of bed, running around or doing something unsafe, it's time to step in. Enter calmly *without saying a word*. Lead them back to their bed, tuck them in and leave. Repeat this process until they fall asleep.

- Don't worry if you find your child sleeping on the floor. So long as they are safe and comfortable enough to fall asleep, there's nothing to be concerned about. Just quietly put them back into their bed. In a few weeks, the novelty will wear off and they'll realize their bed is a far more comfortable place to sleep.

- If your toddler keeps leaving their room when they should be sleeping, install a baby gate on their door frame. It won't stop them opening their door and, if you have a real climber on your hands, they may still be able to escape. But it will act as an extra obstacle, which should eventually discourage them.

- Toddlers have no real concept of time, so are prone to waking up ridiculously early in the morning. To avoid this, make their room as dark as possible using thick curtains or blackout blinds to stop them waking up with the sun. If your child sleeps with a night light, try turning it off when you go to bed so they learn that when it's dark, they stay in bed.

CHAPTER 7

VENTURING OUT OF THE HOUSE

Before you have kids, there's nothing complicated about leaving the house. So long as you're dressed and remember to grab your keys, wallet and phone before you close the door behind you, you're pretty much all set. But add a baby into the mix, and suddenly the simple task of going out becomes a military operation.

Your early excursions will be brief – short walks around the block, to the park or the supermarket, with your baby tucked up tight in your pram or carrier. You won't have the energy for much more than that. Even so, don't underestimate the emotional impact these first escapes will have on your partner. Her protective motherly instincts will be in overdrive as you leave the relative safety of your domestic bubble, so take it slow and be sensitive to her needs.

Before you know it, the nerves will be gone and venturing out of the house will become a daily ritual, albeit one that requires serious planning, logistics and more kit than you can possibly imagine.

The longer you're out, the more you'll need. The sheer amount of stuff you have to take with you for nights away and holidays boggles the mind of every new dad. Of course, you can go away with just the essentials. But if something goes awry (which it invariably does), you won't want to be caught short. Or worse still, be the one who said, "Nah, I don't think we'll need that" when you were discussing what to pack.

To take some of the stress out of this, I've laid out this chapter as a series of checklists, covering everything you need to consider (and bring with you) whenever you leave the house, including why it is important to maintain your baby's routine when you're away from home (my biggest recommendation of all).

The more prepared you are, the more you'll be able to enjoy your days out as a family without having to worry constantly about what you accidentally left at home.

Day trip

Whether you're going out for just a few hours or the whole day, it's best to be prepared for every eventuality. You might have an unexpected nappy blowout, your baby might throw up an entire feed on you or your journey home might take longer than expected, so "less is more" doesn't really apply here.

What to bring for your baby

- Baby bag or backpack – filled with all the essentials your baby might need, including:
  - Spare nappies and wipes
  - Dirty nappy bag to store dirties until you get home
  - A changing mat for your baby to lie on during nappy changes
  - Nappy cream for sore bums
  - Spare set of clothes or two for your baby in case of leaks, spills or throw-up
  - Dribble bibs to avoid milk spills during feeds or if your baby is teething
  - Dummies/pacifiers if your baby finds them comforting
  - Hat – warm ones for colder days and a sun hat with a brim for sunnier days
  - Your baby's favourite comforter (just be sure to keep a close eye on it or strap it to the pram, as losing it could be a disaster at nap time)
  - A few toys to keep your baby engaged and entertained
  - Bottles and formula if your baby isn't breastfeeding (you can usually get boiled water from a café or restaurant when you're out, but, if there's a chance you can't, bring a thermos of boiled water to use instead)
  - A muslin – good for cleaning up spills or protecting your clothes during a feed

- A baby blanket – warm or more lightweight depending on the weather
- Snacks – a useful distraction if your baby has started weaning
- Pram or buggy – to keep your baby safe and secure, for naps and to store all the kit you bring or anything else you might buy during the day
- Waterproof pram cover – in case it rains and you need to keep the pram and baby dry
- Baby carrier or sling – for when your baby gets fussy in the pram, wants to sleep on you or if you need to be hands-free at any point
- Pram cover or a muslin swaddle to lightly cover the pram during nap time

Extra items to pack for yourself

- Water bottle or thermos to stay hydrated
- Snacks to keep you going
- A fold-up waterproof poncho for unexpected downpours

DADVICE

Giving your baby a nap or two in their pram is totally doable, especially if you make it as cosy and dark as possible for them and bring their usual sleep aids to help them settle. But, if you are going to a friend or family's house for the day, it's worth taking a travel cot for your baby to sleep in. They're more likely to sleep longer and better in one of these than they will in the pram, and in the long run, it's good to get them used to sleeping in travel cots.

Night away

Once you've mastered the day trip, you'll soon be ready for a night away from home. Whether staying with family and friends or treating yourselves to a weekend away, these trips are so important, not only for your own mental health but also to get your baby comfortable being around other people and accustomed to sleeping in different environments.

These trips can be quite stressful the first few times you do them (with packing and leaving the house often the most painful part). But if you remember to bring everything you might need and stick to your usual routine as best you can, these mini-breaks from new parenting monotony can do wonders for the whole family.

What to pack

Obviously, you'll need a couple of days' worth of clothes for you and your baby, with spares just in case of any accidents, but other items you won't want to forget include:

- Travel cot and fitted sheet
- Sleeping bag or swaddle and blanket
- Comforter/cuddly toy
- White noise machine
- Muslins
- Baby monitor – so you can enjoy a nice evening without having to constantly check whether your baby is asleep
- Blackout blind to keep your baby's room dark, if necessary
- Thermometer and liquid paracetamol – in case of unexpected illnesses while away
- Bottles, sterilizer and formula (if not breastfeeding)
- Two days' worth of nappies (plus a few extras just in case), wipes and nappy cream
- Waterproof nappy bag to store dirties (if using cloth nappies)
- Baby toothbrush and toothpaste if they've started teething
- Pram and/or baby carrier

Tips on navigating public transport with a baby

- Leave plenty of time if you have a specific train or bus to catch – it always takes longer than you expect to leave the house, manoeuvre the crowds with a fully stacked buggy and get to where you need to be.

- Most buses and trains have designated spaces for prams and wheelchairs, to ensure everyone can travel safely. However, if these spaces are already taken up by other users, you may be asked to wait for the next service or have to fold up your pram and carry your baby instead.

- Don't forget to put the brakes on your pram before the bus or train starts moving!

- If you find yourself navigating lots of stairs on your journey, don't be too proud to ask for help carrying your pram up or down. While you probably can do it yourself, it's not the safest idea and there's almost always another willing parent nearby more than happy to lend a hand.

Baby's first holiday

If anyone deserves a holiday, it's you and your partner. New parenthood is full-on, and a break from the norm is just what you both need. While it won't be anywhere near as relaxing as the holidays you enjoyed pre-kids, just a week or two away from the realities of everyday life will still do you wonders.

Planning your trip

Travelling with a baby is a logistical mission in itself. Here are the main things you need to consider before booking your holiday:

How far are you willing to travel?

The longer the journey and the more modes of transport you'll need to get there, the more exhausted you'll be on arrival. Babies aren't generally good travellers and it's difficult to follow your usual routine on long journeys. Be prepared that your baby may not sleep until you arrive at your final destination, so it might be best to start off with a staycation somewhere close to home.

How baby-friendly is the place you want to stay?

Before booking anywhere to stay, make sure you find out the following:

- Do they provide a cot in your room or will you have to bring your travel cot?
- Is there somewhere you can store milk or facilities to sterilize bottles and make formula?
- If you're taking cloth nappies, is there a washing machine you can use?
- How noisy is it during the evenings and can you get a room somewhere quieter?
- Are there baby-friendly activities in the area?

- Is there a supermarket nearby where you can pick up baby food and other essentials you might need?
- Does your room have a bath so you can do your usual bath-time routine?

How much of a break do you want?

If you really want a proper break from it all, look into hotels that offer a crèche, kids' club or babysitting service. Even just the odd hour of child-free time or a romantic meal by yourselves is worth its weight in gold. Better yet, ask the grandparents if they fancy tagging along – they'll love to be included and there's nobody better to help with childcare.

How do you plan on getting there?

If you plan on driving, add an extra hour or two on to your travel time. Babies shouldn't be in their car seat for longer than two hours at a time, so you'll need to add frequent pit stops to whatever route you take.

If you're going further afield and need to take a flight, this requires a whole other level of organization (see page 202 for the full breakdown). Most importantly, if your baby needs a passport to travel, the application process can be long, so start this well in advance.

What to pack for your baby

You'll be surprised just how much luggage your baby needs. It's not just their clothes you have to pack... it's everything you could possibly need for an extended period away from home.

Unless you know for sure that where you're going has well-stocked shops with all your essentials, you're going to need to take it all with you.

Bulky items
- Pram or buggy
- Car seat (if you're hiring a car or plan on getting a taxi)
- Travel cot (if not provided where you're staying)

Main luggage

- Sleeping
    - Swaddles or sleeping bags (of correct tog depending on where you're going)
    - Comforters/favourite teddies
    - White noise machine
    - Baby monitor
    - Blackout blinds

- Changing
    - Lots of nappies and wipes (more than you think you'll need)
    - Nappy cream
    - Changing mat
    - Washing powder and a wet bag (if you're using cloth nappies)

- Feeding
    - Nursing pillow if your partner is breastfeeding
    - Extra bottles and formula (or a breast pump) if you're bottle feeding
    - Sterilizing equipment if where you're staying has the right facilities (cold water sterilizing tablets are the safest and most lightweight option if they don't)

- Specific items for holidays in the sun
    - Baby swimwear – sun suit or long-sleeve rash vest are ideal for sun protection
    - Swim nappies – non-absorbent nappies designed specifically to catch poo (and prevent you from becoming the least popular person in the communal pool)
    - Buoyancy aids – baby life jacket, rubber ring or armbands, depending on age

- Sun cream – factor 50 SPF or higher from six months of age (any younger and they should stay in the shade)
- Sun hats – you'll need more than one as they inevitably end up getting wet/lost
- Pram cover – to keep the inside of the pram cool for naps (consider also investing in a separate temperature-regulating sheepskin pram liner for your baby to lie on, which are great at keeping little ones cool in hot climates)
- Baby tent – great for beach trips to keep your baby out of the sun and stop them eating handfuls of sand

DID YOU KNOW?

There are great reusable swim nappies on the market today, which means you don't have to take a bulky packet of disposables away with you. They wash well in the basin and are quick to dry, so are an excellent eco-alternative. And don't forget, swim nappies aren't designed to hold pee (only poo!), so should be put on just before going into the water.

Flying with a baby

Prepare for some turbulence when going on a flight with a baby. Even if you have the perfect chilled-out baby who falls asleep easily and has a watertight routine, there's no guarantee this will still be the case once the plane takes off.

It's a game of endurance. You'll have your baby in your arms for most of the flight, so don't expect to read a book or watch the in-flight entertainment. Your sole job will be to keep your baby entertained, happy and calm until you land. Preparation is key to achieving this.

Pre-flight checks

- If you're going on a long-haul flight, you can usually request bulkhead seats and a bassinet without paying extra to reserve them. Even if your baby is too big to sleep in the bassinet, they're still useful as a play area or to give you a break from holding them. Plus, these seats come with extra legroom, which is a luxury you'll definitely want.

- Buy travel insurance. Babies have a special knack of picking up infections and bugs at the least convenient moment, and you don't want to get lumped with huge medical bills on top of your planned holiday costs.

- Get a taxi or lift to the airport if you can. Sorting long-stay parking, driving and then getting a bus to the terminal with a pram, car seat and a million bags is added stress that you don't need.

- Most airlines let you take your normal pram with you all the way up to the gate where they will take it from you and give it back to you when you land (just be sure to take any hanging accessories off the handlebars if you don't want to lose them in transit).

Hand luggage

Most airlines have tight restrictions on the size and weight of hand luggage, but babies are usually allowed their own bag even if they don't have their own seat. You'll definitely need this bag and will probably need to sacrifice space in your own bag for baby essentials too.

What to pack

- Feeding
  - If you are bottle feeding, you'll obviously need all your usual kit. Most airports let parents take milk and other drinks in their hand luggage, without any limits (within reason), which will get scanned when you go through security.

- Lots of snacks
  - If your baby is weaning, you'll need to bring your own baby food, bibs, spoon, and have lots of wipes ready, as it is guaranteed to get messy.

- Changing
  - Your usual fully stocked nappy bag with all the essentials
  - A waterproof, airtight poo bag is essential to avoid stinking out the entire plane
  - Extra wipes
  - Extra set of clothes for your baby
  - Extra set of clothes for you, just in case your baby pees, poos or vomits on you (it does happen!)

- In-flight entertainment
  - For babies, this will just be a selection of their favourite toys (ideally ones that don't roll around, as these could end up at the back of the plane).
  - For toddlers, go for a variety of quiet activities like colouring, stickers, puzzles and magazines. Better yet, put together a special bag of exciting new things to keep them busy.
  - The older they are, the more willing they'll be to sit and watch something on your phone, tablet or the in-flight entertainment system. Don't worry about screen time here – whatever keeps them quiet and engaged is a winner. Just make sure you bring some age-appropriate, comfortable headphones for them to wear.

Checking in

- Ask if the flight is full and, if not, whether you can have the seat next to you kept free to give you some additional space. At the very least, try to get an aisle seat so you can get up and move around more easily.

- Treat the check-in staff like they're your best friend in the world. Pay them compliments. Get your baby to smile at them. Make them fall in love with your little family, and they'll treat you like royalty.

Before you board

- Put your baby in a fresh nappy. It's far easier doing it now than in a cramped aeroplane cubicle.

- Change them into something they usually sleep in, to get them in the mood for sleep.

On the plane

- For take-off, either breastfeed or bottle feed your baby (formula or water) so they are drinking during the ascent. The sucking action helps their little ears to pop, avoiding hours of painful screaming if they don't. If you're weaning, have a fruit puree pouch to hand as swallowing also helps with the ear popping.

- Feeding a baby on a flight is not easy, so try to do this before the catering trolley comes around. On long-haul flights, ask the cabin crew to bring you one tray of food at the start of service and the second at the end. That way, your partner can eat in relative peace while you entertain the baby and vice versa.

- Befriend the cabin crew. They are usually more than willing to hold your baby at certain points to give you a break.

Keeping your baby entertained on a flight

- Give them one toy at a time until they get bored of it before bringing out another, so they don't lose interest too quickly.

- The in-flight magazines and safety instruction manuals are excellent distractions for restless babies (just give them a little rub down with an antibacterial wipe first, as who knows what germs they're harbouring).

- Take the baby for a slow walk down the aisle to the galley area, pointing out every nook and cranny of the plane on your way like it's the most exciting thing you've seen all year.
- Stand in the bathroom together, making stupid faces in the mirror.
- Give your baby to one of the cabin crew or a cooing granny to hold.
- See if they'll watch the iPad or headrest TV for five minutes.
- Stick plasters or stickers on your hand and relax while they spend ages trying to pick them off.

Keeping toddlers calm on a flight

- Wear them out before you leave – walk them through the airport or have a run around to get the wriggles out.
- Travel right before nap time or bedtime, if possible, so your toddler is more likely to sleep on the plane.
- If you have a tablet, load it up with apps, TV shows and movies they like, and don't forget your charger.
- Let them watch videos and scroll through photos on your phone.
- Bring a separate bag of new books, magazines, puzzle books and cheap toys that can keep them going for the whole flight.
- Let them draw and colour on Post-it notes and stick them anywhere they want. They'll love the novelty, plus they are easy to clean up and make minimal mess.
- Don't scrimp on the snacks but avoid anything that may bring on a sugar rush.

DADVICE

If your child is making a lot of noise, it can be stressful, but try not to worry too much. You are doing your best, and remember that many of the other passengers in the cabin will be parents or grandparents themselves. They know exactly what you're going through and are generally very understanding and supportive.

CHAPTER 8

MILESTONES

Over the coming years, you and your baby will go through a lot of firsts together. So many milestones, each one more life-changing than the last, opening up new possibilities (and new headaches) that you'll both need to adapt to.

Some milestones will happen naturally without any input from you. Others may bring tears, take months of practice and require careful guidance. During their first year, your baby will be growing at a rate of knots. Their brain development will go into hyperdrive as they start to take in and understand the world around them, picking up language, thinking and reasoning skills and creating memories. It's also a time when they'll develop social skills, make bonds and build trust while learning how to interact with others. And that's just the beginning...

In this chapter, we'll cover all the biggest milestones during the first three years of your baby's life, with advice on what to expect and practical tips for supporting them through each one.

The big thing to remember is that parenting isn't a race. It's always tempting to compare your baby's progress against other children you know around the same age. But do yourself a favour and try not to. Every baby develops at their own pace. Some may take a little longer than others, but they all hit the key milestones eventually. And rest assured; there are systems in place through your health visitor, doctor and nursery to make sure your child's major developmental milestones are all on track.

My main advice is to try and be as present as you can during these formative early years. There's so much joy to be had in watching your baby's personality start to shine through as they master each new skill. You'll kick yourself down the line if you weren't around to witness it. Finally, don't forget to take lots of photos and videos of every milestone as they happen. When you're old and grey, these are the memories you'll end up looking back on time and time again.

Parenting isn't a race

Just ask any parent,
and all will agree,
that raising a human
is far from stress-free.

You read all the books,
(and some you read twice)
as page after page
gives conflicting advice.

While trying to function
on just four hours' sleep,
and fixing a smile
when you just want to weep...

'Cos few jobs on earth,
feel quite so high-pressured,
where success is subjective
and cannot be measured.

So it's normal to worry,
(and sometimes see red),
when so many babies
seem so far ahead...

While your pride and joy
(though perfectly fine)
just won't hit those milestones,
and seems so behind...

*"Oh wow, look at Ruby,
she sleeps through the night!"*
(While bedtimes at yours
are a 12-hour fight.)

*"And ooh, there goes Timmy
with a mouth full of teeth!"*
(Though yours has just three;
one on top, two beneath.)

*"So Sammie's now crawling?
And standing AND kneeling!!"*
(While your one just lies there,
staring up at the ceiling.)

*"And Fred feeds himself now?!
Ah, isn't that sweet!!"*
(As your baby sits there,
refusing to eat.)

*"Wow, Mylo's now talking,
and counts up to three!!!"*
(When yours only squeaks
if they're watching TV.)

*"And Flo's started walking!
Just look at her go!!!"*
(While your baby's new trick
is picking their nose.)

But hold up, let's stop this;
it isn't a race,
'cos every small human
learns at their own pace.

So let's stop comparing
ourselves against others;
we're doing our best
both as fathers and mothers.

And don't be too hard
on yourself or your baby;
they'll get there eventually,
it's a cert, not a maybe.

As even if everyone else
seems ahead,
they probably aren't
and it's all in your head.

Plus, in a few years,
when this is all in the past,
no one will care
who walked first or talked last.

Milestones checklist

The following list sets out the main physical and mental milestones your baby should tick off during their first 18 months, though take the timings with a pinch of salt. Every baby is different, with their own strengths and personal challenges, so don't stress if they are a bit ahead or behind. At this stage, your love, support and encouragement are all they need.

2–4 months
- Start to smile at people
- Begin to follow things with their eyes
- Turn their head in the direction of sounds
- Recognize and respond to your voice and smile
- Start to reach for toys and objects
- Develop different cries for different needs
- Open and close their hands
- Start to hold their head up when lying on their front

4–6 months
- Start to giggle (not a full laugh yet)
- Reach with intent for toys
- Babble to themselves
- Hold head up unsupported
- Copy facial expressions
- Push up onto their elbows when lying on their front
- Try to roll over

6–8 months
- Laugh
- Recognize themselves in the mirror
- Push arms into clothing when changing
- Reach and stretch for toys
- Copy your gestures and sounds
- Understand simple words
- Stay sitting up with minimal support

- Roll over from tummy to back (not usually a full roll yet)
- Pass items from one hand to the other
- First teeth (though can be earlier or much later)

8–10 months

- Make repeated sounds like bababababa
- Point at things they want
- Early fine motor skills (picking up small items between thumb and index finger)
- Get into seated position unaided
- Fully rolling over without support
- Early stages of crawling (dragging themselves along or shuffling on their bottom)
- Has favourite toys
- More wary of strangers
- Give hugs and kisses
- Hold a bottle and drink from it
- Start to play on their own

10–12 months

- Crawl using legs and arms
- Pull themselves into standing position
- More developed fine motor skills
- Feed themselves finger foods
- Fully formed words like "dada" and "mama"
- Drink from a cup
- Respond to "no"

12–18 months

- Stand up from sitting on floor
- Start to walk (holding on to furniture for support at first)
- Increased vocabulary (just single words at this stage)
- Respond to their name

Growth spurts and developmental leaps

Growth spurts

Beyond the physical and emotional milestones, your baby will also grow a huge amount during their first year, gaining, on average, around 25 cm (10 in.) of height while tripling their body weight. Though this mostly happens gradually, there are certain moments when your baby will experience sudden growth spurts.

While these can happen at any time, most babies follow a similar schedule of growth spurts, which typically take place at:

- 1–3 weeks
- 6–8 weeks
- 3 months
- 6 months
- 9 months

Signs your baby may be experiencing a growth spurt include wanting to feed more often, falling out of their usual daily routine and waking up more regularly during the night. They will of course also gain weight during growth spurts, though you might not notice this. Moving up a nappy size or not fitting into their usual clothes are the clearest signs to spot.

Developmental leaps

Your baby will also go through around ten developmental leaps during their first two years. These developmental leaps are more mental in nature, as their brain experiences exponential growth, using up a huge amount of energy in the process. Suddenly, your baby might get really clingy, not wanting to be put down. They might be grumpy, only happy in your arms. Or their usual feeding and sleeping routines will suddenly go out the window for no apparent reason.

Helpfully, the timings of these leaps are usually pretty predictable, occurring at:

- 5 weeks
- 8 weeks
- 12 weeks
- 19 weeks

- 6 months
- 8 months
- 10 months
- 12 months

- 14 months
- 16 months
- 18 months

Be aware that these timings start from your baby's actual due date. So, if they were born early or late, adjust the leap timings accordingly (for example, for a baby born two weeks early, their first developmental leap should be at around seven weeks old).

Despite knowing this, each developmental leap will almost always catch you by surprise, so keep referring back to this list during your baby's first 18 months. Nine times out of ten, a sudden change in your baby's behaviour will match the timing of one of these leaps, and you'll find comfort in knowing there isn't anything wrong, but rather, there is a scientific reason for what you're going through.

And don't lose heart. Each developmental leap doesn't last for long... usually a matter of days or a few weeks at the very most. As stressful as they can be, particularly if you've just got used to getting a bit more sleep at night, find comfort in the knowledge that they will pass and your baby will get back on track before too long.

DADVICE

There's nothing you can do to hurry developmental leaps along. You just have to wait them out and give your baby all the love and attention they need until each one has run its course. This might mean relaxing your usual routine, letting your baby sleep on you more and going back to feeding on-demand (even if you haven't done that for a while).

Emotional intelligence milestones

As your baby grows into a toddler and their brain starts to process everything they've learned, make a point of tracking any little parenting wins you notice around their emotional intelligence. These alternative milestones are the little pats on the back that every parent needs to show that the life lessons you're imparting to your child are finally getting through:

- Saying please and thank you
- Forming friendships
- Sharing their toys
- Holding your hand
- Giving great hugs
- Asking you a personal question
- Being kind to animals (not poking them/pulling their tails!)
- Playing happily on their own
- Getting engrossed in a book
- Comforting someone who's upset
- Saying "I love you"

"At the end of the day, you don't get a trophy, you don't get a ring, you don't get a banner. But what you do get, if you do it right, is a more loving, kinder, smarter and better version of yourself."

John Stamos

Sitting

If you found the early months of parenthood tiring, you're in for a treat when your baby starts sitting by themselves. You may not realize it at the time, but this brief period before they learn to crawl is one to treasure.

When they can sit unaided, you can surround them with toys and leave them to their own devices for longer periods, giving you and your partner some much-needed time back. They won't depend on you for so much or need to be held so often. And best of all, unlike the later crawling phase, when you put them down somewhere, you know they'll stay exactly where you left them.

Most babies will start to develop enough core strength to sit unaided from between six and eight months, but there are lots of things you can do to prepare them for this essential first step before they learn to crawl and walk.

When your baby is flexible and happy enough to sit in an upright position, and you notice minimal leaning when they are in a sitting device or buggy, try the following exercises to build up their core strength:

- Put them in a seated position with a few cushions behind them and on either side (in case they lose their balance) and get down on the floor with them.

- Place your baby's hands on their knees to make them sturdier and encourage balance.

- Wave their favourite toys around, encouraging them to look left and right, up and down, to get them used to moving their head without tipping over.

- Practise mini sit-ups, carefully rolling them up and down from a lying to a seated position.

- Hold your baby in a kneeling position with some cushions under their tummy and get them to reach up to grab or play with toys on the sofa.

- Try sitting your baby on an unstable surface (like a cushion or sitting on your feet while you support them) so they can learn how to steady themselves.

Crawling

Crawling is a huge physical undertaking for any baby, requiring strength, flexibility and coordination to get it right. But, before even thinking about crawling, your baby will need to build up enough strength in their arms, legs and back to support their full weight. They'll need to free up movement in their hips, knees and shoulders to lift themselves physically off the ground. And just as importantly, they'll need a reason to want to move in the first place.

A baby that spends most of their day in a contained space – whether a carrier, pram, car seat, bouncer, baby seat, highchair or propped up with cushions – will usually take longer to figure out how to move on their own (referred to as "container baby syndrome"). In contrast, the more freedom you give them and the more time they spend lying on their stomach on the floor – otherwise known as "tummy time" – the faster they should learn to crawl.

Step 1 – Tummy time

It's not recommended that you start practising tummy time until your baby has enough neck strength to support and move their head with ease (usually from around six weeks).

When they do, put down a soft playmat and lay your baby on their tummy for a few minutes every day when they are in a good mood (not when they're tired or have just been fed). If they start fussing, don't force it... pick them up or roll them onto their back where they will be more comfortable.

At first, they will just lie there like a beached whale. But, over time, their neck strength and arm movement will gradually improve, and you can stretch out the time they spend on their tummy, introducing toys just out of reach for them to try and grab.

Step 2 – Rolling over

Rolling over will be your baby's first real experience of moving their entire body all by themselves, and it's an exciting milestone. It also has lots of developmental benefits, teaching your baby about balance and coordination, strengthening their muscles and aiding flexibility.

Most babies start to try rolling over from around four months. Rolling from their front to their back usually comes first, though you can help them learn how to roll from back to front with some "assisted rolls". To do this, place a toy just out of reach on the side you want them to roll. When they reach for the toy with their opposite arm, gently support their hips and rock them back and forth until they complete the rolling motion.

By around six months, most babies are able to roll over in both directions by themselves.

Step 3 – Encouraging movement

As natural as crawling is for a baby, it can take some time for them to master this new skill. To give your baby a head start:

- During tummy time, prop your baby up on their hands or elbows, gently applying pressure to their hands, encouraging them to push down and support their own weight.

- Kneel in front of them, holding a toy above eye level, until they lift up their head, neck and chest, arching their back. If their arms struggle to hold their weight, place a small pillow under their chest to prop them up.

- When your baby is lying on their front, gently push their knees forward under their body, so they get used to resting on their hands and knees. In this position, help them rock back and forth, freeing up movement in their hips and back.

DADVICE

While most babies will eventually figure out how to crawl all by themselves, a little help from you will go a long way. Studies have shown that learning to crawl is hugely beneficial for a baby's cognitive development, aiding balance, coordination, problem solving and core strength (all things they will need later on in life). But don't be surprised if your baby has other ideas… many choose to skip the crawling stage altogether, moving around by "bottom shuffling" before suddenly deciding to walk!

Baby-proofing your home

If the sitting stage is a moment of relative calm, think of the crawling phase as tornado season. Because, like a tornado, a crawling baby doesn't discriminate, travels at lightning speed and leaves a trail of destruction wherever they go. Nothing is safe from their natural curiosity. Any cupboard or drawer they can reach will be opened. Anything on the floor will be picked up and chewed. Plus, babies have no real sense of danger; electrical sockets, oven doors, stairs, kitchen knives, hot drinks and precious objects within reaching distance are all fair game, so be extra careful where you leave things.

The minute your baby shows any sign of crawling:

- Put baby locks on cupboard doors and drawers (if cupboard handles are near each other, elastic bands work a treat).
- Install safety gates at the top and bottom of stairs.
- Move cleaning products out of reach or into a locked cupboard.
- Be especially careful with magnets and batteries (especially small disc-shaped ones, which can be fatal if swallowed) and any tiny items that could be a choking hazard.
- Install baby-proofing covers for electrical sockets.
- Clean your floors frequently – any spills or dropped items will end up on your baby's clothes or in their mouth.
- Tie up loose cables, blind cords and wires that could be pulled or chewed.
- Move pet food and water to another room or out of reach.

DADVICE

One of the big adjustments you'll need to make when your baby starts crawling is saying goodbye to any privacy you once had. When they're on the move, never again will you be able to slip off to another room for a little break or moment to yourself. Wherever you go, they will find you...

Can I Please Just Poo in Peace?

If you have a toddler,
who walks or can crawl,
then using the bathroom
is no fun at all.

When all that they want
is to be by your side;
there's nowhere to run,
and nowhere to hide...

Before having kids,
this room was a place,
for brushing your teeth
and washing your face.

For deep relaxation
in hot steamy showers
and lazy hot baths,
that could last for hours.

Or even just chilling out,
sitting alone,
just doing your "business"
while checking your phone.

But now, with a toddler,
it's just not the same,
'cos using the toilet's
now more of a game.

Where you run and hide,
and daren't make a sound,
while trying to finish
before being found.

Each day it will happen;
you're hit by the urge,
to disappear off
for a quick bathroom splurge.

So you put on the TV
and leave them to play,
while (just like a ninja)
you tiptoe away...

To silently sit on
your ceramic throne,
just hoping you might steal
a moment alone...

But then you hear footsteps
outside on the floor,
and a strange creepy scratching
on your bathroom door...

Soon followed by banging
and loud high-pitched cries,
as the loo door flies open
and they burst inside...

To catch in the act,
with a smile or a frown,
one poor pooing parent,
with their trousers down.

But do they then leave you?
By heck, not a chance!
They mostly just stare,
in some weird toilet trance.

As you're forced to finish
in an unwelcome rush,
as your dignity disappears
down with the flush.

So take note, new parents;
if they've not learned to knock,
I'd invest in a baby gate,
and a new bathroom lock.

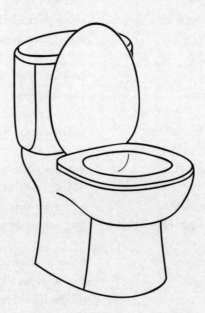

First words

Your baby will start learning how to communicate from the moment they're born, expressing themselves the only way they know how – crying – whenever they want or need something. Over time, their methods of communication will grow considerably, adding burping, sighing, cooing and pulling faces to let you know when they're happy, sad or uncomfortable.

But it usually takes around six months for the muscles they need for speech to develop enough for you to recognize any specific sounds and words. For the most part, everything will sound like adorable, incoherent babbling as your baby figures out how to put two sounds together (and takes great joy in repeating the same ones over and over again).

This babbling baby talk phase is not only extremely cute, but the time when most parents get very excited, as mama and dada are often two of the first recognizable words you'll hear. But don't get ahead of yourself... it's unlikely your baby will be referring to you specifically, and you may find them calling everyone and everything mama or dada over the next few months.

In reality, most babies will only start associating certain words with specific things from around 12 months. And it won't be until your toddler is more than 18 months old before their vocabulary really expands, at which point they can have up to 20 words in their repertoire that you'll understand.

DID YOU KNOW?

Sign language isn't just for babies with hearing impairments. From six months old, you can teach your baby basic signs (such as milk, more, play, change my nappy and pick me up), allowing you to communicate with each other long before they learn to speak.

These timings vary from child to child, but the more you engage with your baby face to face and talk directly to them, the quicker their speech should develop.

A few things you can try to encourage their speech development include:

- Keep a running commentary of everything you do together throughout the day, describing every activity and pointing out and naming anything you see or touch.
- Get up close and personal, chatting with your baby face to face so they can see how your mouth moves as you say different words.
- Sing to them, especially repetitive songs (like "Old Macdonald Had a Farm") or ones with descriptive words you can point to (like "Heads, Shoulders, Knees and Toes").
- Look through books together and point out the pictures, saying what each thing is.
- Start to teach your baby to associate different actions with different words, like waving and saying "bye-bye", putting your hand to your mouth and saying "hungry", or rubbing your eyes and saying "tired".
- Copy the sounds your baby makes and have a little baby talk conversation together. As silly as this might feel in the moment, you'll be surprised how much they enjoy this, listening to what you have to say before replying in their own garbled way.

DID YOU KNOW?

A 2014 study by the Universities of Washington and Connecticut found that one-on-one conversations using baby talk led to better language development in small children. Meanwhile, the more exaggerated the speech and the more variance in the parent's voice pitch, the more one-year-olds in the study would babble, both in response and in general. By the age of two, those babies who had experienced more of this chatter with their parents knew more words than babies who hadn't.

Expanding their vocabulary

Once your baby has learned their first words at around 12 months old, they will still need your support and encouragement to expand their vocabulary through the toddler years. Key here is encouraging them to speak and giving them the confidence they need to learn:

- When you're teaching your child new words, repeat them multiple times in the same sentence to make them stick.

- Ask your toddler where things are in the room or on their body and encourage them to point at them. You'll quickly see what words they know, even if they can't say them yet.

- Keep singing to them, particularly any songs with physical actions and repeated lyrics that they can copy (like "The Wheels on the Bus"), as this will help them remember phrases more easily.

- When giving your child instructions, keep them short and sweet. The more words you use, the harder you'll be to understand.

- Don't criticize or correct them if they get a word wrong, but rather, use the word correctly as part of your reply. Giving them the freedom to practise using words (even if they are made up or incorrect) is far more important than getting them right every time. Once they are ready, they will naturally switch to using the correct words and pronunciation.

- From around two years old, your toddler should start putting words together to form short sentences of two or three words. Help them learn sentence structure by filling in the gaps and repeating their sentence back to them.

First steps

The moment when your baby takes their first tentative steps is one you won't want to miss. It's a huge developmental leap for every child, their transition from baby to toddler, and it's an incredible sight to watch.

Exactly when your baby makes this developmental leap will depend on lots of factors. The biggest one is their personality. If they are fearless, curious, active little things, they'll usually be on the move early. If they are more cautious, happy playing in their own space, they may take a little longer. But generally, by around 18 months, most babies are well on their way to mastering this core skill. Learning to walk usually follows these steps:

Step 1 – Standing

The first step to walking is being able to pull themselves up into a standing position and support their own weight. Most babies start doing this between nine and 12 months, hauling themselves off the ground using furniture or you for support, before bouncing on their legs to build up the muscles and coordination needed to walk.

Step 2 – Climbing

Lots of babies get a big confidence boost when they start crawling, using this new skill to explore previously unseen parts of your home. They will scale furniture, try to climb out of their cot or just clamber all over you, as they figure out how their body works and build up core strength.

Step 3 – Cruising

As they get more confident on their feet, they will soon start walking around the room using the walls, cupboards and furniture for support (referred to as "cruising"). This step teaches them how to maintain their balance while shifting their weight from one leg to the other. Encourage them to cruise along by leaving a trail of toys on the sofa for them to collect.

Step 4 – Assisted walking

Holding your hands or a push-toy for support, your baby will master putting one foot in front of the other while learning how to propel themselves forward. Once they get the hang of this, you can make it more challenging by giving them only one hand for support.

Step 5 – Standing on their own

When your baby can stand by themselves with no support – the ultimate test of balance – you'll know that their first steps are just around the corner. You can practise this together by holding their hands and helping them into a standing position before carefully letting go and seeing how long they can stay up.

Step 6 – Practice makes perfect

Camera at the ready... your baby is ready to take their first steps! Some babies can be a little nervous at the beginning, so make sure you deliver lots of praise and cheer on their new achievement. Equally, if they are looking determined, don't be too quick to offer a hand of support, only helping when needed. It usually takes a week or two for your baby to get to grips with this new skill. Falls will happen, and there may be tears, so always comfort them when they crash land and encourage them back on their feet for another try.

DADVICE

When learning to walk, barefoot is best as it helps to strengthen the muscles in their feet, aids balance and increases their grip on the floor. So, save your money and wait until your baby has started walking before investing in their first pair of shoes. When you do, be sure to buy soft "first walker" shoes, as these are specifically designed for this stage of their development.

Teething

Every baby's experience of teething is different. For the lucky ones, it's possible that they can go through the entire process feeling minimal pain or discomfort. But for most, the arrival of each new baby tooth can bring sore gums, disrupted sleep, difficulty eating and a whole host of unexpected symptoms you'd never expect would be related to growing teeth. Thankfully, though, these troublesome symptoms usually only last for a few days (while the tooth is physically "cutting through" your baby's gums), after which they should ease relatively quickly.

There's no set time when your baby's first tooth will cut through, but the bottom central incisors (bottom front teeth) are usually the first to emerge, from around six months. Most babies' teeth then appear in a pretty consistent order, as highlighted in the diagram below.

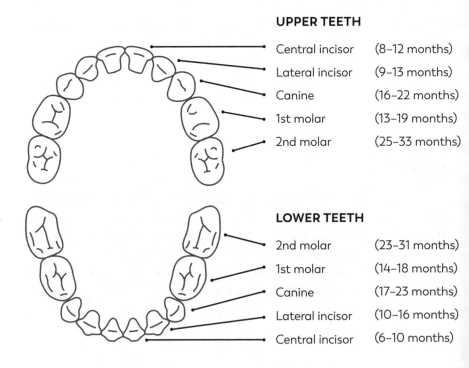

UPPER TEETH

Central incisor	(8–12 months)
Lateral incisor	(9–13 months)
Canine	(16–22 months)
1st molar	(13–19 months)
2nd molar	(25–33 months)

LOWER TEETH

2nd molar	(23–31 months)
1st molar	(14–18 months)
Canine	(17–23 months)
Lateral incisor	(10–16 months)
Central incisor	(6–10 months)

Signs that your baby is teething and a new tooth is making its way through include:

- Putting their fingers in their mouth or constantly wanting to chew things
- Excessive dribbling
- Sore, red (sometimes cracked) cheeks
- Disrupted sleep
- Extra clingy and grumpy demeanour
- Fussiness while feeding or loss of appetite
- Sore bum, and sometimes runnier poos
- High temperature

How to soothe your teething baby

It's horrible seeing your baby in pain, but there are certain things you can do to ease their suffering until a new tooth has cut through, after which any pain should ease:

- Use medicinal products like teething gel (which you rub into your baby's gums) or teething granules or crystals (which dissolve in their mouth, relieving pain).
- Give infant paracetamol if they are in pain or have a temperature.
- Buy teething toys (usually made of silicone, wood or rubber) that are specially designed to be chewed. You can get ones that are filled with a fluid or gel which can be refrigerated, using cold to soothe the painful area.
- If your baby is weaning, avoid any crunchy foods that might aggravate their sore gums (cold cucumber sticks are a real winner).
- A well-timed cuddle always goes a long way.

Tooth care

As soon as your baby has their first tooth, it's recommended that you start gently brushing it twice a day with a silicone baby toothbrush and age-appropriate toothpaste, to avoid plaque build-up on the surface (important as decayed baby teeth can interfere with speech development).

If your baby resists, which they often do, try the following:

- Sit them on your knee with their head resting on your chest.
- Pretend to brush your own teeth first, so they know what to expect.
- Try singing a song to distract them.
- Let them play with the toothbrush before and after brushing so they get familiar with it.

Don't worry if they swallow the toothpaste. Once they're bigger – around two years old – they can usually understand your instructions to spit.

As they get older and more independent, they will likely want to brush their teeth themselves. Let them have a go, but always brush their teeth yourself afterwards to make sure it's been done right. They won't be ready to brush entirely by themselves until they are around seven.

DID YOU KNOW?

You can actually start cleaning your baby's gums before any teeth have made an appearance (though most parents don't have the time!). If you do, use a clean, damp washcloth, a soft silicone baby toothbrush or a silicone finger brush, and gently clean their gums after feeds and before bed. Some paediatric dentists say this can help reduce bacterial growth while promoting good oral health.

Potty training

When and how you potty train your child is entirely up to you. Every parent does it differently and there's rarely a perfect time to start. It requires patience, lightning-fast reactions, a positive mindset and teamwork (so you and your partner need to have the time and headspace to give it a proper go).

When to start

Every child is different. Some will make it clear they don't want to wear nappies anymore. Others may take a little more persuasion. But there are certain signs to look out for that your toddler may be ready to start potty training:

- You notice regular bowel movements at specific times of the day.
- They tell you when they've filled their nappy.
- They are self-conscious about wearing a nappy or having it changed.
- They become interested in using the toilet or potty.
- They regularly remove their nappy themselves (whether clean or dirty).

If you spot these signs and want to give potty training a try, find a week in your diary when you or your partner can be at home and make a plan of action.

Kit you'll need

Thankfully, the kit list for potty training is minimal. You'll need:

- A potty
- New underwear, and lots of it (to get them excited about being out of nappies)
- Loose clothing that your toddler can easily remove by themselves
- Sandals (Crocs or similar so they don't get pee-soaked shoes)
- Antibacterial spray to clean the potty after use
- Night-time nappies

- Training seat that fits inside a regular toilet seat to prevent them from falling in (though training them on an adult seat from the start will save you time down the line)
- A step, so they can get up onto the adult toilet easily

Different approaches

There are multiple ways you can potty train your toddler, but most methods fall into one of the following categories:

All or nothing

Recommended when your child is two or older, this is a popular method for parents who want to potty train their child quickly, as it can take as little as three days to complete.

- Talk to your toddler in advance about what you're planning, giving them a new set of underwear to get them excited about the transition.
- Put any plans on hold so you can focus exclusively on potty training for three days in a row.
- On day one, pack away any nappies and dress your toddler in their new underwear and a T-shirt.
- Show them the potty or toilet, explaining how to use it. Ask them to let you know when they need to "go" and set them the challenge of trying to keep their new pants dry.
- Throughout the day, keep your child well hydrated so they start to learn the sensation of needing to pee. If you're using a potty, keep this nearby at all times for easy access.
- Encourage them to use the potty or toilet regularly, **massively praising them** every time they try or make a "successful deposit".
- There will inevitably be accidents over the three days, so have lots of spare underwear and cleaning products ready to go. If they have an accident, quickly scoop them up and run them to the potty/toilet to finish their "business".
- Stay positive and use accidents as a teaching opportunity, discussing what it feels like when they "need to go".

Parent-led

This is all about sticking to a tight schedule of bathroom breaks throughout the day and can be implemented as soon as your toddler starts showing signs of readiness for potty training. Plus, if your child has multiple caregivers, this method is easy for anyone to follow.

- For best results, ditch the nappies during the daytime and put your toddler in big kid underwear.

- Rather than waiting for them to tell you they need the bathroom, take your child to the potty/toilet at regular intervals throughout the day, staying with them while encouraging them to "go". This can be every hour, or every two or three. The important thing is sticking to the same schedule every day. Alternatively, you can make your schedule more activity-based, for example, getting them to use the potty when they wake up, before and after every meal, in between activities and before going to bed.

- There will still be accidents, but the regular bathroom visits will minimize these and, over time, your child should learn how to "hold it in" and recognize when they need to "go".

- This method usually takes the longest as it's harder for them to recognize their own bodily urges when they aren't initiating the bathroom breaks themselves.

Wait until they ask

If neither you nor your toddler are in any rush to potty train, you can simply wait until they tell you they want to swap nappies for the potty. Usually, this realization comes naturally when they are around three years old after they've observed you and their peers using the toilet and want to join the club.

If you decide on this approach, give the "all or nothing" or "parent-led" methods a try and your toddler should train themselves in record time. Since you have waited until they're a little older, they may also respond well to a reward chart, receiving a sticker or little prize every time they use the potty or have a totally dry day. Save big prizes for when they achieve a whole week without any accidents.

Key things to remember

- Go big on praise every time they try to use the potty/toilet. Your encouragement will be the biggest factor in their success.

- Never show any disappointment, frustration or anger if they have an accident. This will only set back progress.

- Put them in loose-fitting clothes that they can get in and out of easily by themselves and have spares at hand in case of accidents.

- Wash their hands after using the toilet, so they learn this is an important part of the process.

- If your toddler is still resisting potty training after a week, or is getting increasingly frustrated or upset, don't force it. It's better to go back to nappies and try again when they're a bit older.

Night-time nappies

Even if your toddler has been potty trained, they'll still need to wear nappies at night for a while (it's not unusual for kids up to seven years old to use them). Just make sure you switch from conventional nappies to pull-up night-time nappies, which allow them to use the potty/toilet by themselves during the night, promoting independence.

Once your toddler has achieved seven consecutive nights of dry nappies, you can take the plunge and ditch the night-time nappies altogether. There may still be the occasional accident, but nothing a waterproof mattress protector can't handle.

First day in childcare

The timing of this milestone will depend on how much parental leave you and your partner are entitled to, and when you and/or your partner need to return to work. Whether your baby is two months old or two years old, leaving them in someone else's care for the first time will be an emotional milestone for all of you.

If you're lucky enough to have family nearby who can take over childcare duties, this is usually the least stressful option. But for most parents, the only alternative is to leave your baby with a childminder, nanny or nursery. Putting your trust in a relative stranger like this does require a leap of faith, so do your research and make sure you and your partner are comfortable with whichever choice you make.

In this situation, it's common to experience parental guilt and separation anxiety. But the more you can prepare for this day, the less painful this transition should be for everyone.

Separation anxiety

Separation anxiety is normal and can affect both parents and children alike. Adults are generally quicker to adapt to spending time apart from their kids. However, for young children, especially those between the ages of six months and three years, separation anxiety can take some time to even out.

Separation anxiety usually shows itself as:

- crying and screaming before and during childcare drop-off.
- extra clinginess and refusal to let go of a parent at drop-off.
- grumpiness towards a parent at pick-up and in the hours that follow.

Each of these reactions can be extremely upsetting for any parent leaving their child, making you question whether you're doing the right thing. But there are things you can do to get your child more comfortable with being left and reduce separation anxiety.

Preparing for drop-off

Practise before the big day

Going from being entirely in your care to being looked after by a relative stranger can be unsettling for any child, so don't dive straight into nursery without practising some time apart first.

Start off by leaving your child for an hour or two with a family member or close friend in a familiar setting. The objective here is to show your child that they can be safe and happy in someone else's care while reassuring them that time apart is only temporary and you will always come back for them. You can then gradually extend the time you're apart, before leaving them in different settings and with new people. The more often you do this, the easier it will get and the less separation anxiety they should feel when the first day of nursery comes around.

Pack their favourite toys

Being thrown into an unfamiliar situation, it's natural that your child will want to cling onto their main source of comfort at drop-off – i.e. you. But, by ensuring your child has some familiar toys with them, particularly any soft toys or comforters that they know and love, you'll make this transition easier while giving their caregiver an effective tool to calm your child if they feel unsettled after you leave.

Leave clear instructions

If your child has an established routine, specific likes and dislikes, or enjoys certain activities, toys or songs, make sure their caregiver knows about these in advance. The more information they have, the closer they can stick to your child's usual daily routine, removing unfamiliarity and unnecessary stress.

Don't sneak away

As tempting as it might be to sneak away when your child is distracted, try not to. If you haven't said a proper goodbye, your child is more likely to become anxious when they notice you're gone.

Instead, take time to chat with the caregiver to show your child they are someone you know and trust. Then say a happy goodbye, give your child a hug and a kiss, and let them know when you'll be back to collect them, before walking out the door. There may be tears – from them or you – but it will get easier over time.

Be there for your partner

Whatever you're feeling about this major milestone in your parenting life, chances are your partner will be finding this sudden separation from her baby really tough. Don't underestimate the emotional impact this will be having on her, or the long list of worries currently running through her mind.

Try to do the first few drop-offs together so you can be on hand to provide emotional support. Read her the poem on the next page if she's feeling worried or anxious. And remember, sorting and keeping up to date with childcare arrangements is not solely a mother's job, so make it a personal priority to:

- get to know the carers looking after your child and show an interest in how your kid is getting along;
- join the nursery WhatsApp group and make an effort with the other parents;
- help make sure your child has everything they need in the morning before drop-off; and
- share the drop-offs and pick-ups, if you can.

A Poem For Mummy On Her First Day Back at work

You've cared for me tirelessly,
since the day I popped out
and I've loved every minute,
of that, there's no doubt.

But it's time now to head back
to your nine to five;
I know it seems scary, but
I know you'll survive.

Just think of the freedom
you'll have once you're there,
with no nappies to change,
or me pulling your hair.

Like drinking your coffee
before it's gone cold,
and dealing with grown-ups
who do as they're told.

Or grabbing a sandwich
when lunch-hour hits,
without having to chop it
into small bite-sized bits.

And wearing clean clothes
(that I've not yet stained),
while mingling with adults
who are all potty trained.

Plus, I'll be just fine, Mum,
so don't get distraught.
You've prepared me so well
with all that you've taught.

I won't scream the place down;
I'll smile on cue;
I'll eat all my lunch up
and sleep when asked to.

Of course, I'll miss you,
but the hours will fly by...
so be a brave mummy,
and try not to cry.

You've left me in safe hands.
It'll be a right laugh!
I'll fill you in later,
when you give me my bath...

It's time to head off now,
or else you'll be late!
Just try to enjoy it...
I know you'll be great.

I see you're still nervous
but, really, we'll be alright.
So chin up, head down
and I'll see you tonight!

"A MOTHER'S HEART NEVER LEAVES HER CHILD, NO MATTER WHERE SHE PHYSICALLY IS."

Anonymous

CHAPTER 9

RAISING A TODDLER

If you thought looking after a baby was a wild ride, get ready for a whole new rollercoaster of highs and lows once your little one hits the toddler years.

Generally considered to start soon after their first birthday and continue for at least another two years, the toddler stage is a massive step change for everyone. Your toddler is becoming more aware and curious about their surroundings, wanting to explore, touch and taste anything they can get their hands on. They're expanding their vocabulary, learning how to regulate their emotions, and realizing that doing what they're told is nowhere near as fun as doing what they want. Like little sponges, they copy the behaviours (good and bad) of those around them, especially their parents. As a result, you'll need to adjust your own behaviour, being mindful of what you say and do when they're around, checking your emotions while constantly reminding yourself that you're the adult in the room.

It won't come as a surprise to learn that lots of parents, me included, find this stage to be one of the most challenging. Because as cute, cuddly, loving and hilarious as toddlers are, they're also renowned for being little ticking time bombs. You'll hear people talking about the "terrible twos" and "threenagers", referring to just how tricky toddlers can be and their unique ability to push our buttons. But you really can't hold it against them. They're doing exactly what they should be doing at this age.

My advice to you, during these early years, is to spend some time thinking about what kind of parent you want to be for your child. While routines and boundaries are important, don't try to control everything. If you find yourself constantly saying "no" or "don't do that", take a moment to check yourself. Sometimes it's better to save your no's for the times that really matter.

Focus on the positives (which are many) and don't let a little chaos get you down. Make time for them and really listen. Write down the funny things they say. Savour every smile, kiss and hug. Enjoy watching them learn to talk, walk, dance and play. And take pride in the little wins. They're the proof that everything you've taught them is finally sinking in.

Choosing your parenting style

While you can decide for yourself what kind of father you want to be, how you want to raise your child needs to be a joint decision with your partner. For any parenting style to be effective, both of you need to agree on the type of childhood you want your toddler to have, how to talk to them and what boundaries to set.

Once you've made a decision about your parenting style, it's important that you both execute it as a team and stick to it as much as you possibly can.

Different parenting styles to consider

Values-driven

Everyone is born with their own unique personality, which moulds the person they become. But the values we live by are, on the whole, learned from the people closest to us. With values-driven parenting, the aim is to pass on to your child – through your own words and actions – the life lessons and values you think are most important.

Try to find common ground with your partner on the following key questions:

- What are your top three values and why?
- What from your childhood do you want to repeat and what do you want to do differently?
- What do you see as your responsibilities in this family and what do you see as mine?
- What do you want to teach our children about life?
- What's your dream for our family?

Write down your combined answers to these questions and refer back to them every once in a while to check you're showing these values to your child in your daily life.

Gentle parenting

Gentle parenting encourages a positive relationship between you and your child, and follows the idea that kindness allows children to follow rules out of love rather than fear.

The great myth of gentle parenting is that gentle parents never say "no" to their children. As parents, we all need to say no a lot, to stop our kids doing something dangerous, breaking something, hurting someone or just when we don't have time to negotiate. The child of a gentle parent will cry, argue and rebel just as much as any other kid; it's the way that you support them through those tears and help them understand why they got upset that is key here.

There are five crucial elements of gentle parenting:

- **Empathy** – putting yourself in their frame of mind before responding to their actions

- **Respect** – treating your child how you would like to be treated in the same situation

- **Boundaries** – setting simple boundaries that are easy to understand, encouraging open conversations about them and being willing to adapt them as your child grows

- **Understanding** – trying to understand the emotions and feelings of your child, even if they don't have the emotional intelligence to do it for themselves

- **Discipline and praise** – using calming tones rather than shouting as a form of discipline, while praising good behaviours rather than punishing bad ones

Given that most of us adults aren't hardwired to stay calm and level-headed in highly stressful situations, gentle parenting is not easy in practice. But get it right, and you'll teach your child to be calm, to better understand their emotions and to take responsibility for their actions while reducing anxiety and fear.

Hands-off parenting

As first-time parents, it's tempting to wrap your toddler up in cotton wool, avoiding any potential danger, never leaving their side, holding them every time they cry and generally just doing everything for them (often referred to as "over-parenting"). But parenting in this way can create a rod for your back, making your child dependent on you at all times, day and night, hampering their ability to self-soothe, acquire new skills, assess risks and learn independence; all essential skills they'll need as they grow up.

The hands-off approach is a highly effective parenting style usually adopted by more experienced parents who learned the hard way (with their firstborn) the repercussions of "mollycoddling" a child. Putting this style into practice can be done in a variety of ways, including:

- **Don't rush to them when they start fussing** – leave them for a few minutes each time to see if they can find a solution to their problem on their own (rather than always depending on you to do it).

- **Don't hold and pick up your child constantly** – once they're in your arms, they won't want to be put down and will learn, incorrectly, that they can only feel safe and comforted when being held.

- **Encourage independent play** – when they're little, put them on their back on a playmat with some toys or a baby gym to look at while you get on with things nearby. As they get bigger and are sitting up/crawling, don't spend *all your time* playing with them on the floor; back off and let them choose from different toys around them, to make their own fun and develop their imagination.

- **Let them make mistakes** – only intervene if they really are in danger of hurting themselves or someone else.

Gender-neutral parenting

Gender-neutral parenting is simply about allowing your kids to grow up in a home free from the stereotypes that society has established based on gender, giving them the freedom to express themselves and form their own identities outside of their biological sex.

In practice, there are varying degrees of gender-neutral parenting. At the extreme end, there are parents who don't acknowledge the gender of their child until they are old enough to decide for themselves. More common, however, is the softer approach, where parents let their children choose what toys they play with, what colour clothes they wear and what activities they want to participate in – rather than making these decisions for them based on their biological sex.

Routine-based parenting

Setting up and maintaining a consistent routine for your toddler is a lot of work, but it has huge and lasting benefits for the whole family. Like babies, toddlers love the consistency of a routine. It gives them comfort to know what's coming up, when they'll be fed next and when it's time for bed. It'll also help you to plan your own day, know when you'll be busiest, when you can find time to have a break and when you can switch off from parenting duties for the night.

On the flip side, some parents don't like the restrictions that routine-based parenting brings, as it can stop you from going out and doing certain activities for fear of disrupting the routine. But don't let this put you off – routines can be flexed or skipped from time to time, so long as the changes are only temporary. For example, sticking to the usual nap times but doing them in the pram rather than the cot when you're out for the day.

Toddler routines

How you structure your daily routine will be personal to you, depending on your own parenting style and daily commitments outside of the home. Make a plan, focusing on the things in your day that you can control (like mealtimes, naps and the all-important bedtime routine) and leave the rest as TBC. No two days of parenting are the same, so you'll need a degree of flexibility baked in.

Example routines for toddlers

Stay-at-home parent/weekend routine	Weekday routine for toddler in childcare
Wake up (whenever your child decides)	Wake up (whenever your child decides)
7–8 a.m. – Breakfast	7–8 a.m. – Breakfast
8 a.m.–12 p.m. – Play/activities	8–9 a.m. – Childcare drop-off (ask your child's carer to maintain their usual routine while you're at work)
12–1 p.m. – Lunch	
1–3 p.m. – Afternoon nap/quiet time	3–6 p.m. – Childcare collection (this will flex depending on your personal work schedule and childcare provision)
3–5 p.m. – Play/activities	
5–6 p.m. – Dinner	5–6 p.m. – Dinner (either at home or in childcare)
6–7 p.m. – Wind-down and bath	6–7 p.m. – Wind-down and bath
7–7.30 p.m. – Bedtime stories and lights out	7–7.30 p.m. – Bedtime stories and lights out
7.30–10 p.m. – You time (once your toddler settles)	7.30–10 p.m. – You time (once your toddler settles)

Whatever your routine, consistency is key. The more you stick to it, the quicker your toddler will settle into a rhythm and the more predictable their behaviour should be. Of course, there will be days when you have plans and parts of the routine need to be flexed. But try to keep the core timings the same every day, even if that means taking a picnic/eating out or doing naps in a buggy or the car.

Importance of a solid bedtime routine

If you've followed the advice in Chapter 6, your toddler should have a well-structured bedtime routine that carries over from their first 12 months. While some parents gradually move bedtime later as their child gets older, there really is no need to start doing this until long after the toddler years.

DADVICE

Between the ages of one and three, your toddler should still be getting around 12 hours of sleep per night, and (unfortunately) going to bed later doesn't usually mean they sleep in longer in the mornings. So, let yourself have a proper evening off with your partner rather than extending your parenting day longer than necessary.

There are, however, some new elements you can add to your child's bedtime routine as they reach the toddler years:

Pre-bedtime wind-down

It's recommended that you avoid giving your toddler any screen time in the hour before you start their bedtime routine. The blue light emitted from digital screens disrupts the production of melatonin (an essential chemical which causes feelings of sleepiness... something you want your child to have in abundance come bedtime). Instead, prioritize calm activities in the hour before bed, like reading, drawing or going for a walk.

Bath-time ritual

Make bath-time another wind-down event. There's no need to rush it like when your baby was tiny. Have fun together, let them play and chat to them while you wash them and brush their teeth. This is often the time of day when they're most open and chatty with you, so make the most of it.

Story time

Once they're in their pyjamas and ready for bed, sit them on your lap and calmly read a bedtime story together. These stories significantly help with their language development and aid imagination and bonding while signalling that their bedtime routine is coming to an end. Don't be surprised if they ask for the same story night after night – this is normal and actually good for their speech and memory development.

Setting boundaries

Just like routines, toddlers thrive on boundaries (even if they do spend most of their time pushing them to their limits). These boundaries can be big or small, ranging from guidelines on behaviour to physical restrictions that protect them from harm or danger.

It's worth keeping toddler boundaries simple, explaining why they are important and repeating them to make sure they sink in. It's up to you which boundaries you want to enforce, but some examples are:

Behavioural guidelines

- We say please when asking for something, as it's good manners.
- We say thank you when someone gives us something or helps us, as it shows we're grateful.
- We have kind hands and feet – hitting and kicking hurt and aren't nice things to do.
- We only get out of bed at night if we need the bathroom, as it's sleepy time, not play time.
- We say sorry if we hurt or upset someone, as it helps them feel better.

Safety rules

- We walk on the pavement and hold a grown-up's hand when crossing the road, as cars are dangerous.
- We leave our seat belt on in the car, as it keeps us safe.
- We don't touch ovens, radiators, irons or fires, as we will get hurt.
- We stay with our grown-up in the supermarket so we don't get lost.
- We go down the stairs on our bottom so that we don't fall.

When your toddler keeps within whatever boundaries you've set, be sure to give them lots of praise and positive attention to reinforce the behaviour long-term.

Tantrums and how to manage them

Every toddler has tantrums. Loud, emotional, sometimes even violent outbursts, to express when they're unhappy or something isn't right. The first thing you need to know is that these are entirely normal and a natural part of growing up.

Toddlers don't have the years of life experience that we have. They haven't learned how to regulate their emotions yet, or where their boundaries lie. They don't have the vocabulary to explain how they're feeling, or the reasoning abilities to find a logical solution to their problems. These core skills take a long time to learn (a child's brain keeps developing all the way up to the ripe old age of 28), so prepare yourself to deal with a lot of tantrums over the coming years.

Literally anything can trigger a toddler tantrum. Asking them to do a simple task. Stopping them from doing something dangerous. Even just giving them the wrong flavoured yoghurt or the wrong coloured cup. It's nearly impossible to predict when the next one might strike.

Just know that almost every toddler tantrum is caused by some form of extreme emotion or feeling that they don't yet know how to express. To us and the outside world, these outbursts appear to be a child behaving badly. But scratch beneath the surface and it's likely your toddler's tantrum is being caused by something outside of their control.

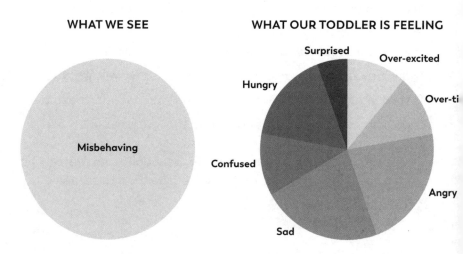

WHAT WE SEE

Misbehaving

WHAT OUR TODDLER IS FEELING

Surprised
Over-excited
Hungry
Over-ti
Confused
Angry
Sad

To avoid a small tantrum turning into a full-blown meltdown, sensitive handling is essential. You'll need patience and a level head (two things that, as tired parents, we don't always have in abundance). This is easier said than done. But the faster you can react, and the gentler you respond, the better chance you have of diffusing challenging situations and getting your day back on track.

How to manage a tantrum

Respond in the wrong way to toddler tantrums and they will last for longer than they need to and reoccur more regularly. Get it right, and you'll be better able to diffuse challenging situations while teaching your child valuable life lessons in how to regulate their emotions.

Our children watch everything we do and learn from how we manage different situations, copying our behaviours, the words we use and even our tone of voice. How we react when faced with a difficult challenge – in this case, a tantrum – will dictate how they deal with conflict in their own lives.

Common mistakes we all make

How we react to a tantrum	What our children learn
Immediately give in to their demands to try and diffuse the situation	If I have a tantrum, I get exactly what I want
Lose our temper, yelling at them to be quiet and stop	Shouting and aggression are effective forms of communication when I'm angry or upset
Send them away to calm down	I don't have anyone to go to when I'm upset
Make empty threats you can't keep	They never follow through so I can do what I want

A better way

The power of distraction – If you sense a tantrum is brewing, try to snap your child out of it early by changing the subject, taking them outside for a change of scene, making a silly noise or doing something completely random like breaking into song or doing a crazy dance. You'll look ridiculous, but it really works.

Calmness is king – Remain calm and say less (this isn't always easy to do, but try whenever you can). Yelling and negative body language only add tension and fear to the situation and will be mirrored back to you in your child's behaviour.

Let them vent – Once a tantrum is in full swing, don't try to stop it. In most cases, they're experiencing "big feelings" and just need to let it all out. Give them the space to do this and they will better learn how to regulate their emotions.

Connect, rather than correct – Don't try and lay down the law during a tantrum. Your toddler either won't hear you or will just dig their heels in. Instead, show some empathy. Come down to their level, acknowledge what they're finding difficult and give them a hug, before waiting for them to come around. Once they have completely calmed down, encourage them to name the emotion they were feeling, so they learn to recognize it for next time.

DID YOU KNOW?

During their biggest emotional outbursts, toddlers are physically incapable of listening and taking in what you say, as their body literally floods with stress hormones, the processing part of their brain goes offline and their "fight or flight" instincts take over. If this happens, assuming they aren't in any danger, give them some space before stepping in and supporting them through the big emotions they're experiencing.

Avoid getting in an argument – When your toddler is old enough to answer back, don't get drawn into a long-winded argument. When you've made a decision, stick to your guns, stay neutral and repeat what you've asked them to do.

Language is important – Be careful what words you use when responding to a tantrum. Small changes can make a big difference in de-escalating the situation:

Don't say	Do say
Stop crying.	Would you like a hug?
Nothing's wrong. You're okay.	How are you feeling?
Because I said so.	Because it's important.
I've told you a million times...	Let me explain again.
Be quiet. Stop shouting.	Please use your normal voice. We don't shout at people when we're angry.
That's it. I'm going to count to three...	Let's take a minute to calm down so I can help you.

Most importantly...

Don't hold a grudge – Once a tantrum is over, don't let the whole experience ruin your day. Move on, stay positive and treat your toddler like nothing happened.

Pick your battles

For your own sanity, if you feel like your toddler is having a tantrum every time you ask them to do something, it's helpful to think about your family rules in three distinct categories:

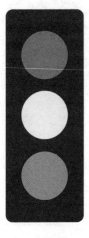

Red rules are non-negotiable (like we don't hit, scratch or bite, we always wear a seat belt in the car and we go to bed when we're told). You never back down from a red rule and you win these battles every time, no matter how long they take.

Amber rules are flexible and depend on the situation (like wearing a coat or eating vegetables). While amber rules will apply on most days, if your child is tired, out of sorts or you're in a rush, you can decide in the moment whether or not to enforce them.

Green rules are "nice to haves" but by no means essential (like staying longer at the park, what to wear or asking for snacks). While you want your child to follow instructions, giving them a bit of freedom from time to time is good for everyone.

It's okay to be angry

Let's not forget that in many situations, anger and frustration are totally valid emotions. Every child needs to learn how to recognize these feelings and channel them in the right way. So, as parents, the aim isn't to teach our children never to be angry, but rather *how* to be angry.

If your child is struggling with regular anger issues, try some of the following activities to help them release tension in a more constructive way:

- Bang drums
- Build a tower and knock it down
- Kick a ball
- Rip up paper
- Listen to music and jump up and down
- Bash modelling clay with a rolling pin
- Blow bubbles

Toddler discipline

Put simply, discipline and punishments aren't actually appropriate for toddlers. They won't fully understand the concept of right and wrong until they are at least two years old. Even then, they probably won't have the language skills to fully grasp why they are *in trouble* until the end of the toddler years. By far your most effective strategy at this age is connection and good communication, which teaches your child to take responsibility and learn from their mistakes, rather than simply complying with instructions out of fear.

Not all behaviours need to be supressed either. You can't blame a toddler for having a tantrum, not listening or failing to follow instructions. They're still figuring things out and need to make mistakes to learn from them. Instead, save your interventions for times when bad behaviours are repeated, are negatively affecting your family life, or when your child risks hurting themselves or someone else.

Age-appropriate intervention

1–2 years old

Between the ages of one and two, toddlers don't need to be told off for doing something naughty or dangerous. They just need to stop what they're doing. Your greatest asset here is redirection.

Try to avoid always saying "no", "don't" or "stop"; otherwise you'll find yourself using these words all day long to the point where they start to lose all meaning.

Instead, make a firm noise, like a loud cough or "uh-UH" sound, to draw their attention and stop them in their tracks. If needed, follow this up with a hard stare, so they know they are being watched and their behaviour has been clocked. In most cases, this will prevent them from taking it any further.

If they continue doing the thing they shouldn't, move them to another part of the room and help them engage with a more positive activity. Give them a puzzle, read a book together, play with building blocks... anything to divert their attention away from what they were doing before.

2–3 years old

From around age two, you can start to introduce the concept of "time out" for bad or dangerous behaviour – pausing whatever you're doing, moving to another area or room and sitting calmly *together* for a minute or two to help your toddler calm down and reset. Don't think of this as a punishment, but rather a moment to connect, distract and get them used to the idea of a cooling-off period.

Doing this together is the most crucial part, as it avoids confusion and a potential power struggle while building trust by showing your toddler that they have your support.

Correcting bad behaviour

When your toddler does something naughty that needs to be more firmly addressed or explained, getting them to really listen and take in what you're saying is the hardest challenge. For the best results, take them to one side and stick to the following do's and don'ts:

DO	DON'T
Come down to their level	Don't stay standing or tower over them
Gently hold their hands in yours and maintain eye contact	Don't speak if they aren't holding your hand or are looking away
Explain why what they did was wrong, speaking slowly and calmly in your normal voice	Don't show your frustration, use over-complicated language or speak fast or in an angry tone
Ask if they understand what you've told them and encourage them to explain it back to you in their own words	Don't assume they've taken in what you told them. If you need to repeat what you've said, do it once more
Offer them a hug and move on together	Don't keep going on about the issue after it's been resolved

Things to avoid

- Putting them on the "naughty step" – toddlers are far too young to grasp this concept.

- Sending them to their room – you want their bedroom to be a safe space, not a prison cell.

- Shouting – this will just encourage your toddler to shout, too, when they are frustrated.

> ### DADVICE
>
> Think about what you are doing and how you react when your toddler misbehaves. If you're always busy and only give them partial, half-hearted attention most of the time, but they get your full, undivided attention when they act out, they will soon learn that misbehaving is the best way to get time with you. To a toddler, a heated interaction is preferable to no interaction at all.

Teaching manners

If you want to have a well-behaved child with good manners, be aware that this is a never-ending job that takes a huge amount of work. It's not something you can nail during the toddler years alone, but the groundwork starts here.

- Make good manners a part of your daily family routine. Remember, a toddler is always watching and listening, so you'll need to lead by example.

- Say please and thank you as often as you can when interacting with your child, your partner, your pets, your neighbours, even your digital home assistant. The more you use these words at home, the more they will become part of your child's daily vocabulary.

- Point out to your child when certain behaviours are good or bad manners, explaining why and praising them every time they show good manners.

It's a tough old slog, but when they do eventually start exhibiting good manners without being prompted, there really is no better boost or validation that your hard work is paying off.

Why won't you listen?!

Toddlers, on the whole, are notoriously bad listeners, which can be hugely frustrating for us parents. You'll ask them to sit up for dinner, tidy their toys away, stop pulling the cat's tail or come in from outside, and your simple instructions will be completely ignored.

As a rule of thumb, don't go on and on repeating yourself, getting increasingly frustrated and raising your voice until your order is eventually obeyed. This will only cause unnecessary stress in your life and won't fix the problem. Instead, try to only ever give an instruction twice. If they haven't responded by then, you need to change tack.

Go up to them, get down to their level and hold eye contact before calmly telling them what you need them to do one final time. This really is the best and often only way to ensure you've really been heard.

> **"Don't worry that children never listen to you. Worry that they are always watching you."**
>
> ———————————————
>
> **Robert Fulghum**

Discovering themselves

The toddler years are a time of massive self-discovery. They'll learn the power of their voice. How to walk, run, play and problem-solve. To say "no" and ask "why", alongside countless other questions that they'll expect you to answer.

As parents, it's our job to give our children a safe space to make these personal discoveries. This isn't a time to "over-parent". Sometimes they will need a lot of support. At others, it's better that they figure things out on their own. Trying and failing is often the best way to learn. Of course, you know your child better than anyone, so it's up to you to decide when to step in and when to stand back.

Build them up

While your toddler is going through this period of self-discovery, try to maintain a supportive and positive family environment. Toddlers are highly adept at picking up the mood in the room, and if they sense you are feeling stressed or anxious, it can be unsettling and knock their confidence. Instead, tell them regularly how proud you are of them. Let them overhear you saying nice things about them. And remind them that you are there for them, no matter what. Toddlers benefit considerably from reassurance, positive reinforcement and praise, so make these key parts of your daily parenting routine.

Supportive phrases to try

- I love you
- Thanks for telling me
- You can do it
- I'm always here for you
- Well done. You really stuck with that
- That's so interesting
- I trust you
- You're so clever
- You should be so proud of yourself
- You kept trying and it got easier
- I believe in you
- You can tell me anything
- Everyone makes mistakes
- Let's figure it out together

Actively listen

Listen intently when your toddler wants to tell you something. As parents, when we're always trying to do ten things at once, it's easy to fall into the trap of "half-listening" when our child talks to us, saying "hold on" or "in a minute". Toddlers really notice this, and it can lead to a range of different problems, including:

- becoming more needy and clingy, craving your attention.
- shouting excessively, as they feel like they aren't being heard (so they up their volume).
- depending on one parent (the one who listens) for emotional support while shutting off the other.
- becoming withdrawn and uncommunicative.

Expand their horizons

Although toddlers can be very opinionated about what they like and dislike, at this young age, they really have no clue. Try to expose your child to as many different experiences as possible, from new tastes and new hobbies to different cultures, people and music.

Toddlers like familiar things, for example, wanting to eat the same meal, watch the same film or play the same game, day in, day out. This is not only boring for you but limiting for them. So, mix things up, involve them in your own interests and try something new together.

Body curiosity

Toddlers are naturally curious about their bodies (and yours too). So, don't be shocked if you catch them poking, pulling or fiddling with their genitals (boys especially), or pointing, prodding and asking questions about yours. If they do, try not to laugh or make them feel ashamed. This is completely natural and harmless, driven by their own curiosity and not anything to worry about.

YOUR WiLLY iS NOT a TOY

Yes, you have a willy,
it's what makes you a boy,
but please be advised, Son,
that thing's not a toy...

At this stage of life,
it's just used for peeing,
so try not to break it
(for your own well-being).

I know it seems fun
and can be a right laugh,
to give it a tug
while you're bored in the bath.

Or how, when you're naked,
it makes you quite happy,
to give it a flick
as I'm changing your nappy.

And how, yes, it jiggles
whenever you cough,
but yank it much harder,
it just might come off...

It's true, when you stretch it,
it does look quite long,
but don't pinch the end, Son,
that's all kinds of wrong...

It may seem small now,
but that's perfectly fine.
Just eat all your veggies,
it'll be bigger than mine.

It's not made of plastic,
so handle with care,
'cos causing it damage
would be a nightmare.

As not much on earth
could be less appealing
than having a todger
with no sense of feeling.

And nobody wants that;
it wouldn't be funny.
You can't buy another
for love nor for money.

Plus when you get older
it'll be much more fun;
I won't tell you why yet
'cos you're only one...

But trust me on this, boy,
when you're big and tall,
your willy will be your
best friend of them all.

Learning through play

We all want our children to get a head start in life, but the toddler years are not a time for structured education. Toddlers' minds and fine motor skills are not developed enough at this stage to read, do maths or write, while their ability to focus on a single task lasts no more than six minutes on average. So, unless you're a trained professional, it's best to leave these life lessons to their teachers when they eventually go to school. By far the most important thing you can do at this stage is encourage your toddler to develop a love for learning through play and quality one-on-one interaction with you. Though it won't seem obvious to them, almost every activity you do together will lay the foundations for their years of education ahead.

Important life skills and the games that teach them

Problem-solving and memory – puzzles, hide and seek, I spy

Word association and language development – story time, singing songs

Numbers, colours and shapes – building blocks, playing "shop", any board games with dice

Following instructions – "Simon says", obstacle course, treasure hunt (with map or using hot/cold/warmer prompts), card games

Fine motor skills – drawing, colouring, arts and crafts, turning pages of a book

Imagination – playdough, craft, building dens, teddy bear's picnic, mud kitchen

Basic science – cooking, planting seeds, water play, building towers

Physical development – climbing, dancing, playing catch, running, riding a balance bike or scooter

Responsibility – tidying up, watering the garden, playing "doctors", feeding pets

DADVICE

Don't feel like you need to be a constant source of entertainment for your child. It's okay for them to feel bored... in fact, it's good for them. Having moments in their day where they aren't being stimulated and have time to let their minds wander inspires creativity, lowers stress, encourages independence, aids motivation and helps toddlers to think more critically.

So instead of constantly coming up with fun things to do, let your child sit with their boredom from time to time (even if they do moan about it initially). You may be surprised what they come up with on their own.

The great screen time debate

There are lots of differing opinions about how much screen time toddlers should be allowed. Usually, people who don't yet have children are the ones who object to it most, proudly saying that when they have kids, they won't be sat in front of the TV or given a tablet or phone to keep them quiet. These are admirable ambitions. But, when the realities of parenting hit, most of us find these standards difficult to maintain.

The more parenting experience you have, the more you will come to realize that screen time is nothing to feel guilty about. Putting your kid in front of the TV may provide your only opportunity that day to have a shower or do the laundry. Giving your toddler a tablet might be the only way to get some work done or take an important call without being asked for snacks. And passing them your phone might be the only option to stop them screaming in the car or on a flight. In all these instances and more, it's not a parental failure if screen time is your go-to.

A few things to consider

- It's recommended that children under five spend less than an hour a day using screens. This may not be realistic for everyone, but use it as a benchmark.

- Set clear boundaries on what shows they can watch and for how long, prioritizing age-appropriate, educational content (that won't overstimulate) as much as you can.

- When streaming, turn off the function that automatically plays the next episode, so they have to ask you before watching another.

- Set parental locks on your devices to stop them stumbling upon content they're too young to see.

- Screen locks are important, too, to prevent them disabling your device or interrupting you every few minutes when they swipe and lose whatever they're watching.

- Putting your devices on aeroplane mode or saying they're broken or have run out of batteries are all highly effective ways to avoid screen time-related arguments.

Co-parenting advice for parents who are no longer together (Al's story)

We're a blended family. When my wife and I first met, we each had a child from a previous relationship before we had one together (our youngest son, Teddy). Over the years, our experiences of co-parenting have been at opposite ends of the scale. For me personally, it's been a challenge like no other. But I know it can be a rewarding experience for dads and, most importantly, the children, if done correctly.

In my job, running a global community and support network specifically for dads, I've come across thousands of dads navigating their way through co-parenting. Subsequently, I've learned a great deal on the subject. Firstly, there are a number of different approaches to consider:

Collaborative co-parenting – Where parents work closely together to make joint decisions about their children's upbringing. They communicate regularly, share responsibilities and prioritize co-parenting as a team effort, aiming to create consistency in rules and routines between households.

Parallel co-parenting – This involves maintaining separate and independent parenting styles and routines in each household. Parents communicate mainly about essential matters related to their children but otherwise maintain a level of independence in decision-making. This approach can be effective when communication between parents is challenging, as has been my experience.

Bird's nest co-parenting – Here, the children remain in the family home while the parents take turns living there. It's the parents who move in and out, allowing the children to have a stable living environment. This approach can provide a sense of continuity for the children but requires significant coordination by the parents.

There's no right or wrong – each situation is unique and every family needs to find an approach that works for them. Once you have, based on everything I've learned over the years, these are my most important recommendations to help you navigate the co-parenting journey successfully:

Always make decisions based on the best interests of your children: Your personal feelings toward your co-parent shouldn't influence the decisions you make concerning your kids. Consult each other on important topics like your child's education and healthcare, and try to make joint decisions.

Prioritize communication: Be open and respectful with your co-parent. Keep each other informed about your child's well-being, activities, school and any important updates. Establish a preferred method of communication, whether through texts, emails, phone calls or a co-parenting app.

Be flexible and compromise: Life circumstances change, so be willing to adapt schedules, routines and responsibilities. Focus on finding a middle ground that benefits your children.

Stay consistent with rules and routines: Collaborate with your co-parent to establish a consistent schedule for contact, school, activities and holidays, as well as similar rules and expectations in both households. This helps children feel secure and know what to expect.

Maintain a positive attitude: Stay positive and avoid involving your children in adult conflicts or negative discussions about the other parent.

Be reliable and punctual: Show up when you say you will and be on time for pick-ups, drop-offs and scheduled activities. Reliability helps build trust and demonstrates your commitment to your children.

Seek professional help if needed: If co-parenting conflicts become too challenging, consider seeking the help of a mediator, therapist or counsellor to help improve communication and resolve issues.

Self-care is important: Taking care of yourself allows you to be a better parent. Balance your responsibilities with self-care activities that help you stay healthy, mentally and emotionally.

In everything I've experienced, successful co-parenting is about putting your children's needs first, above all else. If you do, working together to create a positive and supportive environment for their growth and development should come naturally.

Al is a dad of two, step-dad of one and dog dad to Patch the sausage dog. A passionate supporter of dads the world over, Al is a writer, public speaker, podcast host and founder of Dadsnet (www.thedadsnet.com).

"A CHILD CANNOT HAVE TOO MANY PEOPLE WHO LOVE THEM AND WANT THEM TO SUCCEED."

Anonymous

CHAPTER 10

LOOKING AFTER YOURSELF

I know first-hand how tempting it is after you become a dad to try and do it all and never drop the ball. But, as I've learned from painful personal experience, while it's possible to do this in short bursts, it really isn't sustainable long-term.

As your to-do list grows and grows, you'll have to make sacrifices to keep on top of everything. Staying up late to finish work, cancelling plans with friends, skipping the gym and cutting back on things you enjoy. It's a slippery slope. And before you know it, you'll find yourself exhausted, irritable, mentally drained and at serious risk of burning out.

As admirable as working hard for your family might seem, being a good father and partner shouldn't come at the expense of your physical and mental health. If you're constantly tired, stressed and running on empty, you won't have the energy to be the kind of father you want to be. You'll find yourself getting into arguments or falling ill more easily, knocking you out for days. And worst of all, you'll end up missing out on all the best bits of these early years with your kids, too busy to appreciate just how special this time really is.

While most chapters in this book have been about how to best look after your child and your partner, the coming pages are all about you.

As dads, we have a hugely important role to play in raising our children, and it's essential that we look after ourselves (and each other too). I urge you to consider this chapter and the recommendations within it as essential reading, providing you with the tools you need to avoid burn-out, find a healthy work/life balance, build a stronger relationship with your partner, and know where to go if you ever need help.

Parental burn-out

Burn-out is a state of physical and emotional exhaustion, usually caused by prolonged periods of stress and persistent physical or mentally draining work. With little to no sleep, so many extra responsibilities, plus all the additional pressures we put on ourselves, new parents are especially susceptible to it. If left unchecked, it can have serious repercussions on your health and well-being, leading to depression, loneliness, broken relationships, recurring illness and difficulties bonding with your child. As someone who has suffered from burn-out, take it from me... it's something you want to avoid if you can. Because once it's taken hold, pulling yourself out the other side can be a long, uphill struggle.

But the better you are at recognizing the early warning signs, the quicker you can self-diagnose the problem and make the changes you need to bounce back.

Early warning signs

- Feeling disengaged in daily life, with low motivation
- Short temper, feeling irritable a lot of the time
- Feeling disconnected or intentionally avoiding people
- Not sleeping well
- Stuck in a rut of unhealthy eating and drinking
- No longer looking after your mental or physical health
- Poor immune system, falling ill more often than usual
- Feeling increasingly negative, cynical and overwhelmed
- Getting less enjoyment out of things you previously enjoyed
- Procrastinating and taking longer to get things done
- Feeling helpless, trapped or defeated
- Physical symptoms like headaches, palpitations, shortness of breath and chest pains (**go to your doctor if you experience any of these**)

Bouncing back

Every new parent will experience burn-out in some shape or form during the early years of parenthood. It's important to stress that this isn't a parenting failure or anything to be ashamed of... but, for your own well-being, it is something that should be tackled head on.

If you find yourself struggling, don't just keep ploughing on as you are, hoping that things will get easier on their own. This may happen eventually, but you have no way of knowing when that time will come or the damage you'll do to yourself in the meantime. Instead, make a plan of action, focusing on small, positive changes you can make to your daily routine to feel more like yourself again.

Prioritize sleep – There's nothing better at recharging your batteries than sleep. In the early days of newborn life, clearly, this is not in your gift. But, as your child gets bigger, and you aren't being woken up every couple of hours during the night, try to prioritize sleep as much as possible. While it's tempting to stay up late to get things done or just have some wind-down time on the sofa, head to bed instead, no matter how early it seems. Getting a proper night's rest (ideally eight hours minimum) will do you the world of good and make you better able to face any challenge come the morning.

Get moving – If exercise has taken a back seat while you've been getting to grips with newfound fatherhood, carve out 30 minutes every day to do something active. When we exercise, our body releases endorphins, triggering positive feelings while reducing stress, and there's no better way to bring you out of a slump. If you haven't exercised for a while, don't go in all guns blazing. It doesn't need to be an intense gym session or full body workout. You can start small, with a walk, short jog or some sit-ups. Just try to do something every day so you get back in the habit.

Fuel up for the day – It's easy to fall into bad eating habits when life is hectic. But skipping meals or living on takeaways, though convenient at the time, will only zap your energy levels long-term. If you're going to prioritize anything, make it a hearty breakfast. Your body needs a healthy, filling meal at the start of every day to kick-start your metabolism, keep you going until lunchtime and reduce the temptation to snack. And keep yourself well hydrated too – at least six to eight glasses of water a day.

Technology detox – When you're winding down in the evenings, try not to reach for your phone. Mobile devices and social media are designed to be addictive, keeping you scrolling and staring at a screen for longer than you should, doing your mental health no favours. If you find yourself doing this a lot, set screen time limits on your devices as a reminder to put your phone down and re-engage with real life.

Don't bottle it up – If you're feeling stressed, exhausted or overwhelmed, don't keep it to yourself. Talk to your partner, meet up with a friend or tell a colleague. Putting on a brave face and "toughing it out" won't make anything better. As the saying goes, "A problem shared is a problem halved."

Do something you love – When you spend your whole life working, prioritizing everyone else's needs before your own, it's hard to find the time or energy to do much else. But, if you have a hobby or personal interest that makes you happy, relaxes you or gives you a sense of achievement, don't give it up. Carve out some time – even just an hour a week – to keep this interest going and remind yourself that being a dad is just one part of who you are.

DADVICE

The most important thing to remember is that whatever "you time" you get each day or week, your partner needs at least the same amount (if not more if she's a stay-at-home mum). Getting this balance wrong will only cause jealousy, arguments and resentment, which everyone can do without.

Making time for yourself

As parents, it can often feel like we lose our identity. At home, we're no longer referred to by our actual name, as "daddy" becomes our new calling card. We don't have the time or energy to go out and see our friends as much as we used to. And, when you have a baby or toddler constantly attached to you, the concept of privacy or time to yourself is a luxury we rarely experience.

But, when you work so hard for your family every single day, with hardly any breaks or real time off, it can take a huge toll on your health and well-being (mums and dads alike). Every parent, you included, deserves a proper break from time to time. A little space to breathe. A moment to escape your to-do list and parenting routine and think about something else for a change.

What "time to yourself" looks like	What "time to yourself" definitely isn't
• Going for a run/to the gym • Taking an afternoon nap • Meeting up with friends • Having a lie in • Going out for lunch/dinner • Doing a hobby • Having a massage • Uninterrupted hour to read/listen to music	• Going to work • Having a shower • Doing household chores • Going grocery shopping • Preparing meals • Sitting down to eat lunch • Catching up on life admin • Going for a poo

Ultimately, if you can make a little time for yourself every day (something just for you, which doesn't involve your partner or your child), it will make you a better, calmer, happier parent and partner when your family duties resume.

Finding a work/life balance
(Robert's story)

Before I became a dad, I had certain preconceptions of what building a family should look like... and work often came at the forefront of that.

When my youngest was born, I was in a corporate job, working hard to progress and gaining some awesome wins. Setting up the life I'd always dreamed of for my family. I thought if I worked hard and made wise decisions, that dream life would be set. But I was wrong. I hadn't factored in how the pressure I put on myself to build "that life" would impact me and my family.

Shortly after becoming a dad, I was having a hard time managing a situation at work while trying to keep on top of being the best father and husband I could be. I was sitting in a meeting and couldn't concentrate. At home, my upper body felt painful when I moved. I couldn't sleep as the pain had gripped my chest.

The next morning, I took myself to A&E. By the time I arrived, I'd convinced myself I was having a heart attack. But after a few tests, I was told it was an attack of a different kind. A panic attack brought on by stress. I'd failed. I was stressed and burned out. I'd tried to be the perfect provider, but I'd missed one thing... my mental health.

Managing your mental health as a parent is crucial for your well-being and that of your family. There are so many joys to being a dad, but it can also be demanding and overwhelming at times. After my panic attack, I had to learn and understand my triggers and ways to manage stress.

The thing I neglected when trying to find a work/life balance was the importance of making time for self-care. It sounds so clichéd, but it's the one thing I wish I'd taken seriously from the outset.

Finally taking it seriously has allowed me to be a better, happier father. It's also motivated me to do better at work. Throughout my ten years of being a dad, I've learned some important lessons about finding and maintaining a balance between fatherhood and my career:

- Set clear boundaries between work and family time. When you're at work, focus on work. When you're at home, be fully present, minimizing work-related interruptions. Some of the first boundaries I set were to always have dinner with my family, be there for bedtime and make time to watch binge-worthy TV with my wife. These boundaries can flex from time to time, but once you implement them, it becomes easier to avoid work creeping into family time.

- Prioritize quality time with your family. Remember, building memories isn't always about spending money. Buying your children gifts is not compensation for a lack of quality time.

- Communicate openly with your employer about your family commitments and look at flexible working if possible. This is the biggest thing I wish I had been told. I thought that family and work couldn't clash. But in a world that is more open to flexibility, ask.

- Learn to say no when your plate is full and avoid overcommitting yourself. This took a long time for me, and that's okay.

Despite learning these lessons during my parenting journey, I still often got it wrong. I let commitments at work, at home and in other parts of my life become too much to handle, and I didn't address them for far too long.

Try not to make this same mistake. Ask for help. Do things that make you joyful outside of parenting. Surround yourself with other dads and communicate openly with your support network about how you're doing. These things are all just as important as how you parent. In fact, they will make you the best parent you can be.

Robert is a social impact business owner and dad of two kings.
You can find him on Instagram @robertjdouglas_ and
watch his visual podcast – Pivotal – on Spotify.

Your relationship – tough times and how to get through them

It doesn't matter how close you and your partner are, the pressures of family life will test the limits of any relationship. Parenting is hard work. Arguments, petty irritations and heated conversations are to be expected. It's how you react to them and reconnect afterwards that's most important... not just for your own relationship, but for your child and their future relationships too.

At the end of the day, your child will be more influenced by how you and your partner talk to each other than by how clean you keep the house. They will learn more from how you resolve arguments and apologize to each other than how much money you make. And they will form their own view of what love, respect and teamwork should look like based on how you and your partner interact. So, getting this right is crucial.

Common causes of parental arguments and how to repair them

Feeling underappreciated

Parenting can be a pretty thankless job, especially for stay-at-home parents who don't get paid, don't have an annual appraisal and rarely get acknowledgement for the hard work they put in every day. As dads, we often get the better end of this deal, being congratulated by outside observers just for showing up. On the flip side, societal expectations of mums are generally much higher, adding to the pressure they already feel.

- Make time every day to acknowledge what your partner does and say thank you.

- Don't expect praise for doing essential, everyday jobs unless you thank your partner every time they complete similar tasks.

- If your partner is caring for your child full-time, let them know how much you value what they do. Though it doesn't bring in any financial income directly, the money you'll be saving on childcare and household maintenance costs alone deserves to be recognized.

Lack of sleep

Everyone gets grouchy when they're tired. And there are few times in your life when you'll be as dangerously sleep-deprived as during the first few years of parenthood. Small frustrations turn into big annoyances. Passing comments get blown out of proportion. And if one of you is getting more sleep than the other or, worse still, does something to interrupt the other's sleep cycle (for example, snoring, fidgeting or talking in your sleep), resentment can build, causing friction.

- Get used to saying, "I'm sorry for what I said when I was tired."
- Try not to take things said during tired exchanges too personally. If you both weren't so knackered, they probably wouldn't even come up.
- Agree on a system to share night-time and early morning wake-ups evenly between you.
- Take it in turns to have a lie-in at the weekends, with no restrictions on how late each of you can stay in bed on your designated day. It's often the only way you can make up the hours of sleep you've missed during the week.
- If your snoring keeps your partner awake, don't ignore the problem. Take proactive steps to address it (like changing your sleep position, losing weight, quitting smoking or stopping drinking alcohol in the evenings). If that doesn't work, look into medical treatment at a sleep clinic.
- Don't be offended if your partner sometimes asks you to sleep on the sofa so they can get a good night's sleep – just don't make it a regular thing as this can cause issues of its own.
- If your morning alarms are a problem, get a smartwatch with a vibrating alarm, to avoid waking up the whole house in the morning.

One parent not pulling their weight

When you add a child into your life, your daily workload will increase exponentially. With so many more tasks to complete every day, many of which are small, invisible jobs like meal planning, tidying up toys or calming a tantruming toddler, it's easy for one parent to feel like they're doing more than their fair share.

- Start a conversation with your partner about your relationship, your parenting roles and how jobs at home are shared, agreeing which tasks you'll each be responsible for and which you'll tag team.

- Know your child's daily routine like the back of your hand (including how and when to give them what they need) so you don't need to ask your partner every time.

- Remember that mums often carry most the mental load of parenting, so get involved with the nursery logistics, parent WhatsApp groups, meal planning and potty training so this doesn't all fall on your partner.

- When it comes to domestic chores, don't wait to be asked to do them or "half-do" a job, as this just creates more work for your partner. If you see something that needs sorting, do it there and then, and never assume it will magically get done on its own.

Not listening, poor communication and forgetting to do things

The root cause of tension in most relationships is poor communication. Not sharing your wants, needs and frustrations with your partner until they all come out at once in a massive blowout. Being too distracted by your to-do list, your phone or your own thoughts to really listen to each other. Or only half listening and then forgetting to follow through on something you've said you will do. Every couple has these same issues, but parents more than most, given the sheer number of things on our minds at any one time.

- If something is bothering you, talk to your partner about it (nicely!). They aren't mind readers, so never assume they'll figure it out on their own.

- Don't prioritize work or looking at your phone over connecting with your partner. This just adds to any feelings of neglect and loneliness they may be experiencing.

- Follow through on your promises and let your partner know if you can't, so important things don't get missed.

- Do everything you can to remember key dates and tasks you've been asked to do. "I forgot" is never a good excuse and just appears like you think your partner's request is unimportant. Set reminders on your phone, make a to-do list, write it on your hand... whatever you need to remember.

Loss of intimacy and emotional connection

As parents, it's easy to prioritize the daily grind and put your relationship to one side, focusing all your efforts on childcare and ticking off the endless list of chores rather than giving your partner the support they need. While this effort you're both making is done out of love, the physical intimacy you once had can often take a back seat, causing anxiety, fear, and feelings of rejection.

- Even if you're too tired and emotionally drained for physical intimacy, don't underestimate the power of a kiss, a hug or a foot rub to rebuild connection.

- When giving non-sexual affection like this, it's important that it's given without any expectation that it might lead to something else.

- Don't let the to-do list take priority over showing your partner that they are appreciated and loved. It takes no time at all to stop what you're doing and offer affection, so make sure you do this every single day.

- If quality time is in short supply during the day, make sure you go to bed together at the same time every evening. Staggering bedtimes only fuels disconnection while making any chance of physical intimacy an impossibility.

Four secrets to a solid partnership

1. Learn each other's "love language"

Your love language is how you show love and like to receive it in a romantic relationship. Everyone's love language is unique and often differs when it comes to how you like to give and receive love. It generally falls into five categories – physical touch, words of affirmation, acts of service, quality time and receiving gifts – with most people preferring one type above all others. What you need to figure out with your partner is what your individual love languages are so you can give each other what you each need.

DADVICE

To help you visualize this, here's a real life example. For me, I mainly show my love through "acts of service" (working hard, helping my partner, being hands-on), whereas the way I feel loved is through "words of affirmation" (kindness, encouragement and praise). While my wife also shows love through "acts of service", her preferred love language when receiving it is "physical touch" (hugs, close contact, physical affection). By knowing this, I make an effort to give her more physical attention every day, while she tries to be more vocal in her appreciation. We don't always get this balance right, but we know how well it works when we do.

2. Just apologize

Don't wait too long to apologize after an argument, and never go to bed without trying to resolve it. Delayed apologies just stretch issues out, piling up emotional clutter between you and your partner.

Even if you don't feel like you've done anything wrong, don't let a stubborn sense of pride stop you from acknowledging something you could have done differently or better. So, before things escalate, apologize, ask to start over and try again. It's always better to fix any cracks in your relationship before they cause structural damage to its foundations.

3. Avoid these toxic relationship pitfalls at all costs

- Making passive-aggressive, personal or disrespectful remarks
- Bottling up negative thoughts and avoiding difficult conversations
- Shutting down whenever your partner says something triggering
- Threatening to break up or get divorced during an argument
- Giving your partner the silent treatment
- Withholding your love because your partner upsets you

4. Make time for each other, together

It's a well-researched fact that relationship satisfaction is at its lowest in the early years of parenthood. As modern parents, we're expected to be more attentive to our children than ever before, leaving little time and energy for much else.

But it's okay to prioritize your relationship over your children from time to time. To show your child what a supportive, healthy relationship looks like. To teach them boundaries, respect and patience. That they don't always come first. And to remind you and your partner why you fell for each other in the first place.

Achieving the perfect kid-free date night

- Whether you plan something big and fancy or small and intimate, enjoying each other's company is what matters most.

- Leave parental guilt at the door. The babysitter you've chosen – whether a grandparent or a paid professional – has done this before and will call if there's a problem.

- Make it a "no phone zone". Turn off notifications, set your phone to vibrate and put it in your pocket. The only person you need to hear from is sitting right in front of you.

- Try not to spend the whole evening talking about your kids. They already take up 99% of your mental capacity and you have so much more to catch up on.

- Treat it like a special occasion and indulge. Have another drink, order dessert and don't rush home earlier than needed.

- Don't switch back into domestic mode as soon as you walk through the front door. The chores can wait until tomorrow.

Asking for help (and where to find it)

As a gender, we're far less likely than women to talk about our mental health or consider seeking the help and support we might need. Most of us have been programmed from a young age to behave a certain way. Boys don't cry. Don't be a girl. Man up! But this kind of toxic masculinity does nobody any favours.

Statistically, new dads are significantly more likely than the general population to experience depression and anxiety. And sadly, suicide remains the biggest killer of men under 45. Something has to change.

If you're struggling, don't suffer in silence. Find someone you trust – your partner, a friend, family member, colleague, doctor or other medical professional – and talk to them about what you're going through. Just saying it out loud can make all the difference and is often the first step towards getting the support you need.

There are also countless charities, non-profits and dad-led organizations focused on men's mental health, fatherhood, loneliness, domestic abuse, addiction and everything in between, who can help (for free) if you want more specialist, urgent or anonymous advice.

Dadsnet
www.thedadsnet.com
A brilliant online community and support network, offering advice, support and knowledge for dads who need it.

Andy's Man Club
www.andysmanclub.co.uk
A men's suicide prevention charity, offering free-to-attend peer-to-peer support groups across the UK and online.

MIND
www.mind.org.uk
Free advice and support over the phone and online for anyone experiencing mental health challenges.

Family Lives
www.familylives.org.uk
A charity providing early intervention and crisis support for families, with live chat, a free phone line, email and in-person support.

Postpartum Support International
www.postpartum.net/get-help/help-for-dads/
Offering expert advice, a free helpline that can connect you with local resources and specialist support groups just for dads.

C.A.L.M. (Campaign Against Living Miserably)
www.thecalmzone.net
A charity focused on male mental health, suicide prevention and tackling loneliness, with online resources, a free helpline and webchat if you ever need help.

Looking out for each other

When it comes to navigating the pressures of modern fatherhood, nobody understands what you're going through better than other dads. We're all fighting the same battles, whether we talk about them or not, so it's important that we all look out for each other.

If you see a dad having a tough time, not their usual selves or dropping off the radar completely, check in with him. Ask how he is. If he fancies meeting up. Or just wants to talk.

Hopefully, if you're ever in the same position, another dad will do the same for you.

#DadsSupportingDads

Are you there for Him?

For the dad-to-be,
who must stay strong
when another pregnancy
goes wrong,
who holds it in
for far too long,
ask how he is
and be there for him.

Or the working father,
staying late,
to put food on
his family's plate,
when pressure builds
and becomes too great
would it help him to know
that you're there for him?

To the full-time dad,
the only guy
in a sea of mums
who float on by
without a glance
or even a hi,
don't leave him out.
Just be there for him.

'Cos all it takes
is one kind word
to make a dark day
seem less blurred.
Don't keep it in.
Don't stay unheard.
So ask, listen, talk
and be there for him.

YOU THE DADDY!

Congratulations on making it this far. While you've reached the end of this book, remember this is just the beginning. Fatherhood is a job for life. There will be many more twists and turns on the horizon. New challenges sent to test you. But, with the skills you've learned and the parenting confidence you've gained so far, there really is nothing you can't do.

Before I go, I want to leave you with a few final reminders to take forward on your fatherhood journey:

- Parenting is hard. And, despite what people say, it doesn't get easier. You just get better at it.

- The aim of fatherhood isn't to be perfect. You will make mistakes. We all do. It's how you learn from them and bounce back that's most important.

- No matter how much another parent looks like they have their shit together, behind closed doors, we're all battling the exact same issues. Everyone is just winging it, and you're doing a great job.

- Your time is the most valuable gift you can give your children and the thing they crave more than anything else.

- When your child wants to tell you something, really listen. Because, if you don't take the time to listen to the small stuff when they're small, they won't tell you the big stuff when they're big.

- Your relationship with your partner is just as important as your relationship with your child. You're a team, and parenting is infinitely easier if you work together and appreciate each other.

- If you plan on having more kids, remember that every baby is unique. There's no guarantee that what worked for one will work for the other. Stay flexible, try new things and never stop learning.

- And, as the saying goes, the days are long, but the years are short. They really do go by in a flash. So, embrace the chaos and find joy in the little things. You'll miss these baby years when they're over.

You've got this!

Index

Skin-to-skin 80, 88, 123
Sleep cues 177–8, 186
Sleep deprivation 120, 176
Sleep training 181–3
Sleeping routine see Bedtime routine
Sonograms 31, 129
Speech development 221–3, 228, 246
Spider veins 20
Stages of labour 50–1, 74–8
Stay-at-home parent 54, 129–30, 160, 244, 270, 274
Sterilizing 120, 150, 152, 196, 198, 200
Stillbirth 63
Storage 46–8
  (Of breast milk) 150
Stretch marks 20, 27, 41, 185
Stump (umbilical cord) 36, 42, 84, 105, 112–4
Sudden infant death syndrome (SIDS) 95–6
Support networks 40, 263, 273, 280
Surgery 66–7, 77–8, 84, 120, 138
Surges 38, 58, 74–5
Swaddling 97–9, 172, 174, 177–8
Swollen ankles 20, 27

T
Tantrums 162, 248–52
Tearing 36, 41, 71, 77–8, 84, 120
Teething 117, 144, 148, 174, 194, 196, 226–7
TENS machine 36, 57
Thermometer 43, 117, 171, 196
Thrush 84, 146
Time out 254
Toilet training see Potty training
Tongue tie 147–8, 174
Toxic relationship pitfalls 279
Transition from cot to bed 190–1
Travel 192–205
Tummy time 216–7

U
Urinary Tract Infection (UTI) 21

V
Vaccinations 92–3
Vaginal bleeding 20–1, 62, 66
Varicose veins 20, 185
Ventouse (suction cups) 36
Vernix 80
Visitors
  (Health visitors) 91, 119, 145, 207
  (Other) 121, 125, 176
Vitamin K injection 37
Vomiting 21, 24, 75–6

W
Wait for white 36, 77
Wake windows 123
Walking 211, 224–5
Water birth 36, 68–9, 72, 74
Weaning 153–5, 195, 203–4, 227
White noise 43, 168, 174, 177–8
Work/life balance 132, 272–3
Worry list 22–3

Z
Zinc deficiency 27

Have you enjoyed this book?

If so, why not write a review on your favourite website?

If you're interested in finding out more about our books, find us on
Facebook at **Summersdale Publishers**, on Twitter/X at **@Summersdale**
and on Instagram and TikTok at **@summersdalebooks** and get in touch.
We'd love to hear from you!

Thanks very much for buying this Summersdale book.

www.summersdale.com

Image credits

p.107 © Aleksandra Kirichenko/Shutterstock.com; p.125 © Fox Biz/Shutterstock.
com; p.126 © Strejman/Shutterstock.com; p.147 © Pepermpron/Shutterstock.
com; p.172 – babygrow, vest and socks © Star_O/Shutterstock.com, sleeping bag
© Dreamerr24/Shutterstock.com; illustrations on pp.209, 236, 282 by Marianne
Thompson; p.220 © Yoko Design/Shutterstock.com; p.226 © Double Brain/
Shutterstock.com; p.252 © Hendry084/Shutterstock.com

All other illustrations by Naomi Dawson (no-meillustrations@hotmail.com)